Keeping Customers in Good Times and Bad

KEEPING CUSTOMERS
IN
GOOD TIMES AND BAD

Ronald A. Nykiel, Ph.D.

LONGMEADOW
P   R   E   S   S

Copyright © 1992 by Ronald A. Nykiel

Cover design by Christina Ascione

Interior design by Richard Oriolo

ISBN: 0-681-41192-9

Printed in the United States of America

Edition

0 9 8 7 6 5 4 3 2 1

To my wife, Karen,
for encouraging me to write the book.

To my son, Ron, for his suggestions, research,
and efforts all along the way.

A special thanks to Kathy
for her help in this endeavor.

ACKNOWLEDGMENTS

In November of 1990, the first International Quality Service Summit was convened in cooperation with President Bush's Special Advisor on Consumer Affairs, and co-sponsored by John Hancock Financial Services and AT&T. At this event, many outstanding individuals shared their thoughts for achieving service excellence in the 1990's. During the summit, a number of interrelated topics emerged. These included customer satisfaction, quality service, global competition, the marketing relationship in creating expectations, and the importance of employee and customer feedback, to name a few. It became evident that keeping customers in good times and bad required more than a quality process, more than a marketing effort, more than motivated employees—it required an attitude set by leadership and formalized throughout an organization. It required a focus on customer needs and appropriate actions. These thoughts led to this book.

Therefore, I am indebted to Stephen Brown, President and COO, John Hancock Financial Services, and Randall Tobias, Vice Chairman, AT&T, for their leadership in co-sponsoring the summit. I express a special thanks to those true quality leaders who presented their many ideas and thoughts. These include Edwin Cooperman; Richard Marriott; Alita Holut, First National City Bank of Chicago; Shirley Lanier, TIAA-CREF; David Roe, USAA; Robert Galvin, Motorola; and other presenters and participants.

Special appreciation goes to Jim Collins and Bob Cardillo of Avis, Charles Aubrey and Lisa Wente of Banc One Corporation, John Norlander and Sue Gordon of Radisson, Jeff Davis of Davis Frame Company, Roy Wilson and Linda Palmer, Pearle, Inc., all of whom made contributions to the case examples.

A special thank you to those who provided me the opportunity to learn more about service leadership: Bill Marriott, Chairman and CEO, Marriott Corporation; Juergen Bartels, President, Carlson Hospitality Group; Bob Stetson, President and CEO, Pearle, Inc.; and Joe Vittoria, Chairman and CEO, Avis.

CONTENTS

PREFACE

In today's marketplace, offering a quality product or service experience is no guarantee you will attract or retain customers. Likewise, providing a variety of sales or purchase incentives doesn't necessarily convert consumers to customers. There is more competition everywhere, be it in your product or service category or for alternate uses of the consumer's monetary resources. Decisions are not limited to choices between brand A and B, but also whether to spend on something else or save.

Achieving success in service or sales starts with understanding the customer and knowing how to respond. This is easier said than done. Given product or service parity, why do some succeed and others fail? What makes a customer prefer your brand to another? How can you be sure your business practices are meeting the market's needs? When are your employees helping or hurting you attract customers? What can you do to better the odds at both keeping existing customers and adding new ones in good or bad economic times? How do you outperform your competition?

There is no single answer or set of answers to these questions. But what successful organizations and their managers have in common is that they are able to read and respond to the needs and desires of their customers. Moreover, they are able to convey this understanding to their employees. And, in doing so, they have their employees respond appropriately at the point of encounter with the customer. By meeting the needs and desires of the consumer, they convert one-time consumers into loyal customers.

Understanding the customer, motivating the employees, and communicating with responsive messages are all important characteristics of those successful at service and sales excellence. The interrelationship of these seemingly distinct functions is what forms an overall organizational environment which leads to success. The common denominator is recognition of the customer as the unifier. So let's start with understanding more about customers.

I

. . . .

UNDERSTANDING CUSTOMERS

Studies show that it costs you five times as much to attract a new customer as it does to retain an existing one. In today's business world, most companies are scrapping for every possible customer. This book will present a number of ways how you can find new customers. But its major focus is on customer retention. After all, not only is keeping customers more financially expedient, but every time you find, condition and sell a new customer, you've got to take steps to keep that customer too.

A quality service or product is always a major factor in any company's success. The companies that are the most successful, history shows us clearly, are those that also know how to treat their customers right.

PRECONDITIONING

Understanding your customer is as essential to providing on-target service as it is to closing a sale. It is important to understand the customer's needs and wants in order to position your product or service sales message in line with the customer's expectations. Even if all of these considerations are explored, there is still the base-level conditioning of the customer's attitude that you need to take into account.

Today more than ever, customers' attitudes have been preconditioned. Many are cynical about service and service personnel. Price changes, unmet promises, and encounters with poorly trained workers have all contributed to this preconditioning. Everyday experiences often reinforce this preconditioning, resulting in customer cynicism.

This preconditioned cynicism may be the result of many other factors as well. Attitudes and beliefs learned from parents and peers, societal events, personal experiences, accumulated and current circumstances in life all precondition consumers' attitudes.

How do you capitalize on this preconditioned consumer to convert him to a purchaser and a repeat customer? What should your sales pitch say to be believable? How should your point of encounter employees respond? Well, it all depends on specifically how that customer has been preconditioned. It also depends on the motivating factors driving that consumer. Is it price? Is it service at a price? Is it ego? Is it efficiency? Is it one or all of these factors, or a multiple of other reasons? One thing we do know—whatever it is—this preconditioning projects itself into customer attitudes that the attuned salesperson or marketer can read clearly.

ATTITUDES

Sometimes you can "see" an attitude. Picture someone walking up to a hotel check-in desk with a reservation confirmation slip of paper in his hand. What do you think his preconditioned attitude is telling him? What do you think he expects might happen if he didn't have that confirmation number and printed slip of paper? Now picture a person striding towards her bank teller, holding out a countersigned check and ID card. Do you think this person wishes to dawdle and engage in a leisurely conversation? Does she want to hear about all the bank services available?

It doesn't require a Ph.D. in psychology to understand the signals being sent by consumers. But knowledge of human nature is necessary to help us recognize and respond to these signals. Think of the people who represent service excellence to you. The smart company sends out a marketing message that is able to meet a wide range of preconditioned consumer needs.

Attitudes can be influenced prior to, during, and after the actual sale. Those influenced by the quality of the service or product and the flux of the buyer-seller relationship are called "internal." "External" attitudes are less under your control, but can be just as important in the successful service of your customers.

Internal influences include everything from the initial marketing message to the actual service offering or product itself. The marketing messages shape an expectation. This expectation will either be raised or lowered upon initial contact with the service or product. Let's take as an example an advertisement that promises a full-size or luxury automobile for a weekend rental. If the advertisement shows a Buick, the consumer will not feel fulfilled with anything less than a Buick. The consumer's expectation will be further reinforced upon arriving at the rental car lot, if he sees several Buicks awaiting. His expectation may even be raised if he also sees several Cadillacs in the lot. However, if he sees only mid-sized and compact cars, his expectations will be lowered and any cynical preconditioned attitude will be reinforced. Note, his attitude and expectation levels have been shaped before he meets or talks with any point of encounter service personnel.

External influences have nothing to do with your pre-sell messages or service/product offering. Take, for example, the teller who extends a pleasant greeting only to encounter an irate "Can you move any faster?" or consider the front desk clerk who says, "Welcome," and is met with silence, a credit card, and a look that says "One mistake and I'll make you regret it." The teller doesn't know the customer received a ticket for speeding only five minutes prior. The front desk clerk has no idea the guest was delayed four hours because of an overbooked flight. These service personnel have to know how to deal with customers who have just gone through a severe attitude-changing experience.

The behavior of the consumer is preconditioned by both the messages you send and by the external influences received prior to the purchase experience. Knowing what to say in your messages and how to handle the unexpected attitude are but two of the keys to keeping customers. How the consumer's attitude has been preconditioned is a variable that both marketing and service must constantly monitor if you are to achieve service excellence.

REACTIONS

How the employee reacts to the customer's behavior becomes the pivot point in the game of keeping customers. If you react personally to an irate individual unfairly attacking you because of an external influence of their attitude, that will likely result in a "lose-lose" scenario. To play the game of service excellence requires reacting with the emphasis of acting. A good actor goes by the script and when necessary improvises. A good service employee learns to "act" according to a response script and, when required, takes on authority to resolve problems.

Not everyone is capable of controlling and modifying their reactions. Some individuals can truly adapt, pretend they're on stage, and perform flawlessly under most any attitudinal barrage. Others react to the first volley with a volley of their own. When this occurs, it is usually a customer lost forever.

One key to controlling or modifying a reaction is to have the proper training. View the road to keeping customers as a game or play. You need the rules or script to win. You might find a great improvisor, but that is the exception. The rule is training.

RESPONSES

With proper training, you can convert reactions to measured responses. You can meet hostile attitudes with disarming phrases. Just as the actor who trains becomes flawless in the execution of his lines, so, too, will the service employee. The satisfaction of a good performance, of winning the audience or customer over enhances the work environment and enriches the individual psyche.

There is no single course or bible of reaction/response phrases that provides all the answers. There are too many individuals, attitudes and circumstances to deal with in virtually any business. But there are helpful ideas to be garnered from the plethora of materials available. Empathy training can be a major key to the many steps needed to keep customers.

It may come as no surprise, but not everyone is capable of a controlled response or trainable. Some individuals are bad actors. They just do not have the bravery, the split-second timing, or the psychological make-up to go on stage. Others, akin to uncoordinated dancers, will consistently step on the customers' toes with their responses. So, before you sign everyone up for empathy training, take the time to assess their likely success at servicing or selling. Consider their attitudes and personalities. Are they of a nature that allows them to step into the actor's part? Can they respond to attacks peacefully—neither lashing back at the customer, nor tormenting themselves by holding in all their anger? And, do they possess the ability to bounce back after momentary reflections and respond with the poise of the good actor?

Empathy training helps in the reactionary process to recognize and respond to diffuse the negative and reinforce a "bond" between customer and employee by selecting the proper response. In point-of-encounter service situations, the selection of the appropriate response results in keeping the customer or customer satisfaction. The wrong response results in the likelihood of losing the customer. While this sounds simple, there are pitfalls along the way to be avoided. These include one of the biggest of them all—failing to communicate the importance of winning to your employees.

You will never be successful at service excellence or retaining customers until your employees understand why their winning performance is so essential. You will dramatically increase your odds of winning back existing customers and closing sales if you also remember to communicate rewards (verbal, written, or financial) to those who performed well. After all, isn't that what a true performer expects and lives for—the recognition and reward?

MOVING TARGETS

Today, more than ever, customers are a moving target. Attitudes are changing and understanding how to deliver quality service means you must see the customer's point of view. This means you must have a customer orientation throughout all your customer service programs and practices. You must also have a sales message which causes the consumer to be responsive and select your product or service.

In examining where customers are coming from, you have to put yourself in their shoes. You purchase many companies' services and products. What has your personal experience taught you? One of the first things you must have discovered is that quality service has become rare. Over the years, thousands of people and companies have loudly claimed their quality, but how many have actually delivered? Even companies that have managed to live up to their claims later scaled back their efforts, some in order to achieve more profitable operations, some out of a lack of will or loss of purpose.

Any number of firms have cut costs, eliminated manpower, deleted training expenses and other supportive efforts that assure a quality delivery system. Many of these firms have not changed their overall marketing message or promise of quality service when talking to the consumer. They put their sales personnel under greater pressure to perform with less product/service delivery support. Few people simultaneously make these cuts while claiming improved quality service, but in the end, the customer gets less actual delivery, and this leads to consumer dissatisfaction.

The toughest place to judge consumers' attitudes and the quality level of service and products is always your own business. Experience helps, but cannot be relied on solely. Where do you begin to get a current and true fix on your customers and their attitudes? There are a number of information-gathering techniques you can employ. The most important start is for you to have an objective and on-going approach to customer feedback.

LISTENING AND OTHER TECHNIQUES

The basic customer feedback technique is called *listening.* At its most rudimentary, it consists of a customer talking—or even *not* talking—and you figuring out what he really means. There are other techniques. They range from simple informal mechanisms to complex long-term professional services. What works for you largely depends upon the size and complexity of your business. Here are some of the techniques and services which may help you:

Comments/Complaints Form   The easiest and least complex type of feedback process is a "comment card" or complaint form. A simple review of these on a regular basis will reveal areas where problems are becoming serious. Repeat complaints should immediately make your priority list. One of the most important things you can do is seek the customer's name, address and phone contact on these forms. Most people are preconditioned to believe that it's not worth their time to complain because no one ever responds. If you do respond and do so fairly, instead of losing a customer, you may be on your way to retaining one.

Questionnaires   Questionnaires are an extension of your comments form, with a greater number of probes for key areas and the opportunity to quantify results for trend analysis. Also, you can use questionnaires to identify new opportunities. The key to questionnaire usage is to make sure the questions elicit truthful, valuable answers, and to judge the responses in more than a superficial manner. People are usually happy to tell you what they think; why they think that is much harder to derive.

Customer Service Index   Often referred to by many different names such as quality delivery index or customer relations profiles, a customer service index provides an ongoing quantifiable measurement of your comments or questionnaire feedback. Their measurements can be viewed by time periods, geographic area, stores/operating units, etc. In more progressive firms, such indices serve both as an awareness mechanism as well as a motivator to perform. Some firms establish healthy competition between units and use "scores" as a means of reward.

Focus Groups   Sometimes questionnaires or comment cards only provide surface clues or trends which need further qualification. Focus groups are an excellent technique when more in-depth probing is required. Focus group research should be conducted by qualified professional organizations. There are many benefits for using professionals, beginning with the actual design process, to use of trained moderators, to the data interpretation and applications.

Shopper Services   These are firms who provide a comprehensive program of purchasing your product or service offering and reporting back to you on their findings. This service can be invaluable at helping you spot major and minor problems in your delivery, and a variety of employee-related problems you might be unaware of in your operations. Some firms will even provide mystery shoppers who reward your employees for superior service on a surprise basis.

Customer Perspective Audit   One of the most comprehensive techniques to understanding the total of your customers' perceptions is to have a "customer perspective audit" conducted. This analysis begins with your pre-sell messages (advertising, packaging, promotions, etc.), and continues through the entire customer relationship process to the post-sell follow-up. The CPA usually begins with a comprehensive audit/check list which goes item by item through all point of encounter interfaces with the consumer. Conducted properly, this process may impact everything from your advertising to your billing and sales procedures.

Gap Analysis   While the customer perspective audit will provide you with an indicator of your total quality/service delivery process, a gap will always exist between the results of these findings and your own or management's opinion(s). A Gap Analysis utilizes quantitative and qualitative research methodologies to take a "perception reading" of both your own management's perspective of its quality service delivery and the consumer's perspective. For example, on a scale of percentages, the consumers' ratings may be at 60 percent (fair performance) and management's may well be at a 90 percent rating (excellent performance). Thus, a 30 percent gap is evident between what the customer is experiencing and what management believes it is delivering. Through use of focus groups and some of the other techniques described, the reasons for the gap and, more important, the solutions to close the gap can be identified.

* * *

There are more techniques and forms of quantitative and qualitative research available. The important point is that listening to your customer is critical to offering excellence in service delivery and to keeping customers. It also helps you attract new customers by identifying their needs. Careful listening will also let you target your marketing messages more precisely. Most important of all, you should receive the information you need to take appropriate action.

ACTING

What you learn from these various feedback mechanisms might be categorized into two types of findings. First there's the knowledge that is nice to know but not going to help you keep or retain customers. The second type is knowledge that is usable and will help you in your business activities. Obviously it is important to discriminate between the two, and try to attain as much as you can of the second type. Look for findings that suggest change in these areas:

Pre-sell Message Signals Are your customers telling you you're not addressing their needs or over-promising? Is your pre-sell image in line with the consumers' perceptions? Is your pre-sell message competitive or a strong enough motivator to cause action? Are your pre-sell messages being sent to the right target(s) with the right content? Are they sent frequently enough?

Purchasing Process Is the point of encounter easy to reach or do you have too many roadblocks? (Roadblocks might be: phones that ring too long, hours that are too short, staff that doesn't have the answers, lack of selection choice, inflexible pricing or payment policies, etc.) Once the consumers have reached the point of encounter, will they find it pleasant and efficient? Simple things like cleanliness, appearance and elimination of hassles are very important to the consumer. Keeping people waiting needlessly loses customers more easily than checking them out efficiently retains them.

Are you taking inventory of the customer's payment? Are you doing it efficiently? Are you offering the customer the choices of payment *they* desire versus what you want? It always amazes me to have my American Express card out, ready for prompt point of purchase payment, and to be asked: "Would you prefer to use Mastercard or VISA, or open a store charge?" NO! Why are you wasting my time and irritating me? What is even more amazing, is when you get the same question and you're paying with cash in your hand.

The point of payment is a sensitive moment. Sieze the opportunity. Compliment the customers on their purchases and efficiently accept their payment. Listen to what they tell you—whether it's about the product, their buying experience, their frustration, or how happy you have made them.

Post-Sell Strategies Think of your last five purchases and ask yourself, did anyone offer you a reason or incentive to come back or purchase again? Now, think about your own business—your last five point of purchase interfaces. Did you make any offer or provide any incentive? What are you providing that customer as an incentive to return? Do you have a process installed to follow up and ask your customer if they need more help or are satisfied with their purchase experience? Don't let your competition outsell you at this point—or they'll retain not only their customers better, but yours as well!

In summary, understanding your customer is the first and most important step toward keeping customers in good times or bad. Recognizing their current attitudes may well be premised on preconditioned reactions to events and experiences. Don't react, respond after listening. Taking the time and using appropriate listening techniques will result in useful steps to help you meet the consumers' needs and fulfill their expectations. Your product/service delivery system from pre-sell to post-sell will be in line with the current needs of the consumer. And your sales messages and motivators will be on target. The results will be a quality service and sales experience that will please both you and the customer. For now, you have converted the consumer to your customer.

II

· · · · · · · · · · ·

PERFORMING TO KEEP CUSTOMERS

TYPES OF CUSTOMERS AND THEIR SIGNALS

mployees should know how both to *listen* and *view* customers. Just as psychologists and behaviorists are trained to read expressions and gestures, so too can the point of encounter employee. Customers continually send signals, some friendly and some hostile! These signals provide rules as to when or how to respond, and call for appropriate actions.

Most who have put in their time on the front line at the point of encounter have their own nomenclature or categorizations of customer types. The categories and labels may vary, but the signals sent are universal. While it is virtually impossible to describe all varieties, here are some types of customers you may well identify with and tips on how to deal with them.

Fast Freddie   Look for the man in motion, arms outstretched, wallet or credit card in hand, heading full steam ahead toward the point of encounter. In his office, he is the multiple paper, phone line and meetings specialist. Fast Freddies want you to move with the speed of lightning, anticipate their needs before they speak, and to respond instantaneously. They don't want to hear "I'll be with you in a minute." They want you to run their charge card through in record time so they can be on their way.

The best way to handle Fast Freddies is to be polite, efficient and, if you can, keep them busy during the sales transaction. Don't take their time, unless it's focused on expediting their departure. Fast Freddies love efficiency and can't tolerate slowness. To win a sale, ask them to help expedite the process; they are likely to pick up the pen and sign the contract. On the other hand, drag-on (or overkill) is likely to result in their saying they just have no more time and will have to get back to you another day. Sale lost!

Watch for them. They are coming through your front door right now.

Slow Sally   Friendly, warm, and conversationally oriented, Slow Sallies are the opposite of Fast

Freddies. Slow Sallies view the point of encounter transaction as more of a social event than a process. They tend to view the point of encounter employee as a new-found friend and want to exchange pleasantries. Indeed, Slow Sallies want the conversation to go beyond the pleasantries to more time-consuming topics. Slow Sallies want you to reply, but more importantly, want you to listen. The actual sale or transaction is secondary to the "event." For Slow Sallies, this "event" is what the day is all about. They like people—especially those who will let them talk and show interest.

Slow Sallies can be among your best repeat customers. You just need to recognize that it is worth your while to take your time with them and that they really will purchase.

Of course, Slow Sallies come in both sexes. They can be found most often in areas where retired and elderly people dwell.

Loud Larry   Happy or unhappy, Loud Larries want everyone to know they are there. Loud Larries want attention, recognition, and to be the center of the transaction. To some degree, the transaction is also a social event, but one at which they are the center of attention. When happy, Loud Larries want all to know *that* they are buying, *what* they are buying, and from *whom*. This event can be a happy occasion, like a wedding. However, when Loud Larries are unhappy or feel they have been wronged, they also want the whole world to know.

Encouraging Loud Larries to talk about how much they like the goods, service, or treatment is like a radio commercial on full blast. You may as well take advantage of the free air time and reply and respond on cue. When Loud Larries switch to the boisterous complainer, efficiency and turning down the sound become priorities. Take care of their needs and dismantle their attacks immediately. Your instantaneous reply and right response will tone them down.

In fact, if your policies are flexible enough, give a Loud Larry just about anything beyond what he expects and he will revert back to the positive radio commercial with the push of a button. If you want to close a sale with a Loud Larry, consider using him as a testimonial in some fashion. Remember, he likes to hear, see, and read his name. You may just find an insatiable repeat customer and, at a minimum, a loyalist out pitching your brand with a vocal broadcast. Word of mouth works, and Larry's got a big one.

Lost Lucy Lost Lucies can be spotted looking around and give the appearance of being preoccupied, in a daze, or directionless. She probably doesn't know what to ask, or how to start.

A simple "May I help you?" or "What can I do for you?" may be enough to get a Lost Lucy to open up her mind and focus on what you want them to—buy your product or service. A harsh, curt, or complicated reply will cause a Lost Lucy to slide back into the other world.

Lost Lucies want to be guided through "protective space" with minimal external encounters. If you can provide that environment, you will keep and retain a loyal customer, for they will feel comfortable in your non-pushy environment. If you are too aggressive, they will flee with the wind.

Poor Paul   While similar in appearance to Lost Lucy, Poor Pauls aren't lost, just spacy about what to do. They are generally interested in what's going on at the point of encounter or point of sale, but need a little help.

Poor Pauls like explanations, road maps and, most important of all, sympathy and affirmation. Reply with reinforcement of the choice they are about to make. Assure them that this *is* the correct choice and direction in which they should go. While they still may feel unsure, your encouragement and methodological rationale will help them affirm in their own way that the purchase was the "right decision."

Poor Pauls want you to fix it for them—make them feel better. The same is true with respect to returns. Poor Pauls walk in, goods in hand like a wounded animal and seeking help. Take charge. Take those goods from Poor Paul and tell him everything is going to be all right. You're on your way to winning a friend and long-term customer because you understand.

Defiant Dan   Born to be obnoxious, Defiant Dans just don't want an answer or deal. They want it their way or else. Look for the immediate challenge, a call to the consumer protection organization, Better Business Bureau, to be signals sent by Defiant Dans. They don't care about your refund or rebate policy. "Here is what I want" is their favorite phrase.

Defusing a Defiant Dan requires timing, listening, looking for the window of agreement, and moving to respond. Try to find a point where you can say: "Dan, I agree with you that the policy is not right in this instance, and I am going to work with you to go around it." Defiant Dans love to enlist help. So, be their help if you want to keep them as a customer or close a sale. If necessary, invent a rule you know you can break and then do just that. Break the rule for only them!

Many times, Defiant Dans want the next level up. They view that first point of encounter employee as the appetizer and their objective is the manager or vice president—the main course. Very rarely do Defiant Dans want to go for the icing on the cake, the president, because Dan knows this is where the intimidation may not work. So, save Dan the dessert decision and give him something to help him believe he set you, your company, and the whole world right. Amazingly, Defiant Dans who believe you helped them right a wrong become loyal customers and, yes, broadcasting friends.

Threatening Thelma   As a child, it seems, Threatening Thelma's first complete sentence was, "You'll be hearing from my lawyer." The second sentence is, "Let me see your supervisor or a vice president."

Threatening Thelmas come in two distinct looks. One is the signal broadcaster look, glasses down on the nose and finger pointed, even before any words escape the mouth. The other look is tight-lipped and squinty-eyed, ready to kill.

Reply with extreme patience and few words. Listen or ask questions until Thelma's adrenaline level has dropped. Reply in an antagonistic manner, or even give off the wrong facial expression, and the war is underway. No matter how battered you get, respond with a genuine politeness, professionalism, maintaining your composure (or if you prefer, cool), but don't dare be indifferent. If you can enjoy your own ability to handle the attack, reply as indicated.

Threatening Thelmas eventually blow off their steam and see you as a person. Thelma will shift her vengeance to the product, the process, or someone else. When you see the meltdown, seize the moment to solve the problem or resell Thelma. Unlike Defiant Dans, Thelma will only return because she feels guilty about how she may have injured you initially. You now have a return customer, for better or worse.

Impatient Irene   A distant cousin of Fast Freddie, Impatient Irenes send all kinds of signals and clues. Look for fidgeting, motion, finger tapping, pen rolling, watch watching, and eyes roaming.

Most Impatient Irenes already know the solution to their problem or key to selling them something. So, wait to reply until they complete telling you the way it should be resolved or sold. If you can respond in the affirmative, do so promptly and resolve the problem or close the sale. If you have to respond differently, or want to, start with phrases like: "I can get you a refund or replacement faster if . . . ," or "I can have the goods to you faster by . . . ," or, best of all, "Let me take care of it like this . . . and you can be on your way to more important things."

Impatient Irenes feel two strong motivating forces. One is urgency, and the other importance. These individuals view small things most people take for granted as urgent issues and have a strong sense of responsibility and, thus, importance about all they are doing. So, stroke their egos and serve them efficiently, and they will return as customers time and time again.

Cautious Carol Cautious Carols are often spotted reading labels, scrutinizing ingredients, putting on their glasses, unpinning wrapped shirts, and holding items up to the light. These visual signals are frequently followed by a lot of favorite questions: "Is it returnable," "What if it doesn't . . . ," and "Will it be . . . ?" Cautious Carols are concerned individuals. They want perceived quality, genuine value and no mistakes. Moreover, they need to feel satisfied, be reassured, and told they are making the right choice. Cautious Carols are not bothered if a little more money is involved.

Replying should be factual and reassuring. Where possible, cite others who have made the same decision and were highly satisfied. Cautious Carols usually have to answer to someone—a boss, a spouse, or their other self. They fear both criticism and rejection. They crave being praised for the right and prudent decision.

If you are successful at making a Cautious Carol receive praise from someone else—especially that significant other—you will have one of the best repeat customers on earth. Cautious Carols will view you as a friend and trust will build into loyalty as they continue to receive positive feedback on their purchase decisions.

Returnaround Rhonda   Returnaround Rhondas are easy to spot with package in hand or with the request to try it "on loan." Usually amiable, Returnaround Rhondas seem like your best customers. Unfortunately, they only purchase once and are constantly exchanging or trying another.

There are two types of Rhondas. First, the non-malicious Rhonda who simply can't make up her mind, or frequently changes her choice. The second is the devious Rhonda who is out to beat the system by wearing your product, using it, or whatever, and then either returning it or exchanging it.

The first Rhonda can be turned into your best customer with polite agreement. You can sell her more expensive choices, if you can convince her the new ones are much better than the original. A sure way to sell the non-malicious Rhonda is to provide her an incentive—percentage off, or two for one, or any other offer on her new choice. A simple "Aren't you lucky, Rhonda? Your new choice is on sale today!" will be enough to close the sale and keep the customer.

Unfortunately, there are a lot of "beat the system" Rhondas out there. They distinguish themselves from the other Rhondas because they are very aggressive and occasionally offensive when returning an item—and always right. You *know* they wore the clothes, used the goods, paraded around in the jewelry, etc.

If you believe this Rhonda is worth keeping as a customer (some are not), go with the story/flow and accept the return or make the exchange. You may as well be as nice as you can about it. Your other choice is to see if you can entice them into non-returnable purchases—once in a lifetime bargains they can't refuse. Sometimes in a moment of weakness they buy for real.

Avoid challenging or arguing with the "beat the system" Rhondas, for they can quickly become Threatening Thelmas.

Social Sam   If only point-of-encounter employees weren't paid by the hour, we would all love Social Sams. They're friendly, warm, outgoing, genuinely sincere, and very talkative. These nice fellows make point-of-encounter employees learn the concept of empathy by practicing it in reverse. You can spot Social Sams with their slow paced walk, penchant for browsing, and frequently seeking your point-of-encounter employees' advice. The advice sought may be on the items to be purchased, but more likely it is on everything from doctors to Lotto numbers.

These renowned story-tellers do buy and are good repeat customers to those who listen and take time with them. In fact, they are truly offended by any too-efficient or curt employee. As strange as it may sound, efficiency and promptness scare Social Sams. So, if you want a Social Sam as a customer for a long, long time, be ready to look at the photographs of the grandchildren, dog, cats, or hear about the son or daughter. You can always sell them something for one of their favorites if you are quick to say, "You know, your grandson would just love this . . . and it's on sale!"

Sold!

Important Irving   See a person looking around to see if others are looking at him and you have just found an Important Irving. Observe the person who beckons you across the room, aisle, or crowd when you're behind a counter or obstruction and you have Mr. Important Irving. Important Irvings want the world to know they are important; they want you to come to them, and to be treated as royalty. These are the characters who rake leaves with a sport coat on, go to a fast food restaurant wearing $200.00 shoes, and don't understand why everyone else can't change their vacation or schedule to their convenience. So, as you might expect, your point-of-encounter employees need to spot Important Irvings and reply immediately.

Responses must be delivered with crisp "yes, sir" efficiency. Never tell an Important Irving the goods are on sale because of a small defect. Important Irvings view defects, coupons, and damaged packaging like diseases. On the other hand, Important Irvings can be easily sold, especially if you stroke their egos.

You should never say "That is a fine jacket. It looks very good on you. We sold a few of these just last week." Important Irvings do not want to be lumped together with anyone else. A sure closer would be phrased like this. "Mr. Important Irving, this is made of the finest material available. In fact, this is the only jacket of this high quality and unique design that our store received. It certainly does compliment your physique. I will have our tailor . . ." Be sure your tailor also is clued in and approaches with a slight bowing motion and says, "Mr. Important Irving, your physique was made for this jacket. Let me just adjust it here. I will do it immediately if you like."

And if you want to keep Mr. Important Irving as a repeat customer, be sure when he is leaving the premises he overhears you saying to all, "That Mr. Important Irving just purchased that magnificent, unique jacket everyone admired."

Career Cathy Today, more and more of your customers are career oriented. A Career Cathy knows it is important to "look the part" so you can spot Career Cathies in their neat business attire and fashion designer clothes. Career Cathies are usually looking for prompt, competent and efficient service. They hate not being recognized as "management" or executives. All point of encounter personnel should be on the bulletin distribution list to look out for Cathies. They are your present and future customers. If you don't believe it, just analyze who most of the auto makers, cosmetic companies, banks, clothing firms, etc., aim their advertising at these days. Career Cathies are a major purchasing force.

Respond with efficiency and equality. If you wish to keep Career Cathies for the future, give them a reason to return. Reasons can include new lines, a more sophisticated model, or price specials. If you have a Career Cathy working for you, ask her help in training others to understand how to handle Career Cathies.

You will be sure to lose a Career Cathy as a customer and infuriate her if your point-of-encounter employees are condescending, overly chummy, or simply out of tune. The most out of tune example I saw was on a plane when a stewardess asked a male executive "What may I get for you and the little lady?" In fact, "the little lady" was the company president and the male executive was one of her managers.

Junior John To some extent, Junior Johns are much like Career Cathies. Junior Johns have cracked the ranks of management right out of graduate school. They have new-found powers and rights, including the right to purchase and be treated with respect. Unfortunately, some Junior Johns get a little carried away with it all and become a combination of a Loud Larry and Mr. Important Irving. You can quickly spot Junior Johns, for they look like Career Cathies—well groomed and clothed during work hours. They have a sense of education and learned sophistication about them. You can expect them to inspect, be intelligent purchasers, and be somewhat demanding.

Respond with facts, figures, and product/service knowledge. Don't treat a Junior John as a young man; that may bring out the Mr. Important personality. You'll have lost a customer permanently. Don't be fooled by Junior John's straightforward and often friendly approach. It is his opening personality. If you reply with the high-tech knowledge expected and with the level of respect demanded, you will in all likelihood win a customer and make a sale.

This transaction will lead to a trustful relationship built on respect.

Occasionally, you will encounter the obnoxious "I have money/credit card" Junior John. Enjoy your controlled performance, inflate their egos and take their money!

The world is complex, and while most consumers will demonstrate some of the traits of these above described characters, you can probably add your favorites or new ones to the list. What is important is that you recognize the process that leads to keeping customers and closing the sale. The process is:

Look for Signals

↓

Assess When to Reply

↓

Respond with the Right Approach/Words

↓

Close the Sale

↓

Keep the Customer

WHEN TO REPLY

The hardest part about selling is listening. Listening requires concentration, patience, assessment, and timing the reply. The customer characters described require different timing and different reply approaches. When to reply and listening are skills developed from experience. These are difficult to teach. However, if you can get the initial clues, take an initial assessment and tentatively identify the character, you are on your way to winning timing. Reply timing ranges from instant to very measured, depending on the character. The following schematic may be of help to you in assessing when to reply.

When to Reply Chart

Consumer	Instant	When Asked to or On-Cue	Very Measured	At The End
Fast Freddie	X———X			
Slow Sally				X———X
Loud Larry		X————————X		
Lost Lucy	X———————————————————X			
Poor Paul	X———————————————————X			
Defiant Dan		X————————X		
Threatening Thelma		X—————————————X		
Impatient Irene	X———X			
Cautious Carol	X———————————————————X			
Returnaround Rhonda	X———————————X			
Social Sam				X———X
Important Irving		X———————————X		
Career Cathy	X———————————X			
Junior John	X———————————X			

HOW TO RESPOND

There are no magical words or responses for every situation. All I can offer are some general guidelines on your approach and tone of response. How you respond will either ultimately keep or lose that customer, make or break the sale. Just as reading the customer, looking at the cues, and timing the reply are a learned process, so, too, is how to respond. Practice will inevitably be of great value.

Here are some general suggestions on how to respond based on the consumer characters just described.

How to Respond Chart

Consumer Type	Suggested Response Techniques/Approaches
Fast Freddie	Be brief. Reach for their card, cash or form. Show movement. Give them something to do like "sign here."
Slow Sally	Be friendly. Listen. Speak slowly. Ask questions.
Loud Larry	Use their names. Move efficiently. Complement them. Never argue.

Lost Lucy	Show empathy. Reassure. Provide suggestions. Help decide.
Poor Paul	Provide clear choice. Help with decision. Reassure them of the decision.
Defiant Dan	Maintain your cool. Say as little as possible. Seek a point of agreement. Be efficient.
Threatening Thelma	Say as little as possible. Move quickly. Keep cool. Be polite.
Impatient Irene	Be fast. Ask a question that flatters them. Be brief in speech. Keep in motion.
Cautious Carol	Provide assurances. Extend help in the decision process. Reinforce doubts. Provide hope— "It's going to be just right!"
Returnaround Rhonda	Expedite the process. Provide a value-added incentive. Give options. Show appreciation.
Social Sam	Listen. Reply in detail. Relax. Don't rush anything.

Important Irving	Call by their name. Flatter their ego. Treat as if royalty. Recognize their desire to be first, the best, and unique.
Career Cathy	Be efficient. Don't be overly chummy. Recognize their importance. Use sincere flattery on their choice.
Junior John	Show respect. Appeal to their egos. Provide facts when asked. Give a reason to return.

WHAT TO SAY AND NOT TO SAY

For everything you should say, there are numerous statements which should never cross your lips. One of the best ways to learn these and remember the important do's and don'ts is to associate some key phrases with the consumer character types described. Here are some suggestions and examples which should help you win customers and close sales, as well as prevent you from losing the transactions.

What to Say and Not to Say Chart

Consumer Character

Fast Freddie

Do's

- Let me take that for you right now.
- I'll call in your card while you're signing.
- Would you like this sent to save you time?
- I'll put them on hold.
- Let's see how fast we can ring this up.

Don'ts

- I'll be with you in a few minutes.
- I hope the lines aren't as backed up as last time.
- Let me refold this and box it. . .
- Let me take this call.

Slow Sally

Do's

- That is very interesting. Can you tell me more?
- Would you like me to show you the other models?
- Let's talk about that. . .
- What do you think?

Don'ts

- I'm in a hurry, so let me take that right now.
- No use wasting time, let's. . .
- That's nice (she just told you her aunt died in a car accident and you weren't listening).
- Let's see how fast I can get you out of here.

Loud Larry

Do's

- Mr. Loud Larry, you look great.
- How much weight did you lose?
- You are correct. . .
- Right away, Mr. Loud Larry!

Don'ts

- Are you sure it was this way?
- I'm not going to agree with you.
- Keep your voice down.
- When I get the time. . .

Lost Lucy

Do's

- Let me help you with that.
- Why don't we look closer at this one.
- I'd be thrilled to receive this.
- What a wise decision!

Don'ts

- Let me know when you make up your mind.
- It's your choice. . .
- I'm not sure, but it's your call.
- You can return it. . .

Poor Paul

Do's

- This is the better choice.
- You have selected the best deal.
- You are much better off with that one.
- You can't miss. What a great decision!

Don'ts

- You decide. It's a toss up.
- There are some other deals we could offer.
- This one's cheaper. It might do the job, but. . .
- They can always bring it back if you were wrong.

Defiant Dan

Do's

- I agree, it's wrong.
- Let me correct that now.
- I'm going to see if we can't get that policy changed.
- I'm sorry this happened.

Don'ts

- That's your point of view, however our policy is. . .
- I can see this is going to take some time to explain to you.
- Since you have a problem, let me take care of this first.
- (Say nothing and turn your back or shake your head.)

Threatening Thelma

Do's

- Let me get this cleared up immediately.
- I'll take care of it.
- I'm sorry this happened.
- You're absolutely correct.

Don'ts

- Why don't you tell me all your problems with it?
- Well, if you didn't . . .
- These are made very well. You must have. . .
- I'll have to get back to you. Please wait a minute.

Impatient Irene

Do's

- I'll put that in the box while I ring it up for you.
- Let me take you first.
- You have a great tan. I'll have you back in the sun in two minutes.
- I've stamped your ticket. Just take the exit to the left to avoid the line.

Don'ts

- I'll look for a box. Be back in a minute.
- As soon as I finish this last inventory item, I'll be right with you.
- Wouldn't you like to fill in this application for. . .
- We have to redo the sales transaction. I forgot to . . . Do you mind waiting?

Cautious Carol

Do's

- You can be sure with this one.
- It has a super guarantee.
- What a great buy. You were lucky.
- I'd be proud to receive this.

Don'ts

- If it breaks, you can return it.
- That's the last one.
- I couldn't tell you. Perhaps someone in shipping will know.
- You either love these or hate them.

Returnaround Rhonda

Do's

- Let me give you this one. I'll take care of the paperwork.
- Would you like to select another, or a refund?
- You know the step-up model was just reduced.
- We could exchange it for the better one.
- Thank you for coming back. We'll make it right.

Don'ts

- I have to process the return, so you will need to fill these out.
- I don't believe you can return that item. I'll have to check.
- Can you come back when we're less busy?
- Was this worn, used, etc . . . ?

Social Sam

Do's

- Take your time. By the way, that is a very good looking tie.
- Well, Sam, tell me more about that . . .
- You have an excellent perspective on that.
- Come back soon. I want to get brought up to date on this.

Don'ts

- Have you made up your mind?
- While you're deciding, I'll take care of . . .
- You just keep looking. I'll be back in a few minutes.
- You can read up on it. I don't have time to go into it now.

Important Irving

Do's

- Mr. Important Irving, we are so pleased to see you.
- I have had this reserved for you. There is only one like it.
- Absolutely stunning.
- Everyone will be envious.
- It is the best I have seen.

Don'ts

- We have plenty of those models in stock. It's your choice.
- I sold one just like it to Mr. Not As Important.
- Do you know Mr. Not As Important? He works with your company.
- Here is a practical item. (This translates as a "common" item).

Career Cathy

Do's

- Exquisite and practical choice in one.
- Most people do not have your excellent taste.
- This makes a very important statement.
- This is the best table and view in the restaurant.

Don'ts

- So, how is the job going?
- One of your co-workers bought that version.
- I'll be back. Let me take care of this gentleman first.
- How about back here? It's a great spot.

Junior John

Do's

- Fine choice. It has superior technical features.
- Mr. Junior John, would you prefer the table with a view?
- Very nice suit. Mr. Important Irving had a similar cut on the other day.
- Thank you for staying with us. Please use this complimentary upgrade to our suite floor on your next stay.

Don'ts
- I'll be with you in a minute, young man.
- You don't need a bell-man, do you?
- In addition to our gour-met restaurant, we have a coffee shop.
- How about over here near the speakers?

When to reply, how to respond, and what to say, or not to say, are the keys to any transaction. While the examples provided were largely focused at the point of encounter in a retail or service transaction, the process can be applied to any business, point of encounter, or consumer character. Through actual experiences, role playing, and situation analysis, you can learn to enjoy the challenges and perfect the performance. The rewards are keeping customers, closing the sales, and building repeat business.

CUSTOMERS, CUSTOMERS, CUSTOMERS

KEEPING EXISTING CUSTOMERS

Regardless of what your product or service offering is, retaining existing customers is usually the most efficient manner in which to have sales. Existing customers have many choices and can never be taken for granted. Today, you must not only perform to keep the customer, but also need to give existing customers a reason to return. You lose customers for many reasons, some your fault and some due to external circumstances. So keeping customers becomes a dual strategy of eliminating your faults and providing overwhelming reasons to have the customer re-select your brand.

Brand loyalty is extremely difficult to achieve due to the introduction of many new choices, a fiercely competitive marketplace, and a constantly moving consumer target. Why do some brands weather all the storms and others go by the wayside? Is it product/service quality? Is it pricing flexibility? Is it new innovations? The answer is never simple. Frequently it takes a number of tactics and strategies to achieve the objective. To simplify this, let's focus on the key steps to customer retention. These can be categorized in three strategy groups. The first deals with all those things we send as signals to our customers which form a level of expectation. You might say, what you do sets yourself up to win or lose. If you promise the customer too much (more than you deliver), the result will be dissatisfaction. If you promise too little or don't give your customer enough of a reason to re-attract them, they simply won't come back. And, naturally, if you do nothing—no call, no ad, no letter, no reminder—you are likely to be forgotten.

Let's look at some tactical pre-sale or pre-point of encounter strategies which bring customers back. Here are a few:

- Reminders: a thank you note or call
- Special offer: e.g., "on your next visit, receive. . ."
- Up-dates: tell them what's new, improved, waiting for them when they return
- Trade-ups: offer to take back a previous purchase as part payment for a new or more expensive one

• Free merchandise: to customers only, receive X, Y, or Z absolutely free as a valued customer

Pre-sale strategies from a marketing perspective range from direct mailing to direct visits (sales calls).

Never underestimate the power of a coupon. The world, and virtually every market segment on earth, loves coupons. Their usage has reached an all-time high. In fact, it has been reported most consumers feel they are not getting the best deal unless there is a coupon involved. As one researcher put it, we have retrained the consumer in the basic purchase transaction. It now begins with the coupon.

The second set of tactics which form a strategy group are at the actual point of encounter—the execution phase. Studies have demonstrated if you have a miscue at the execution level, seven out of ten customers won't even tell you. They just won't come back. And, of the three who tell you their expectations were not met, two will switch brands. What you can do at the point of encounter is, at a minimum, deliver what your marketing message promised. What you ideally want to do is deliver more than promised or expected. The result will be a satisfied customer who can be reminded to return. How you achieve this "delivery plus" concept largely depends on the nature of your business. The formula is simple:

Promise 85–95%	Deliver 95–100%	= Customer Satisfaction
Promise 100%	Deliver 99% or less	= Lost Customer

The more you exceed your promise and can afford to do so, the higher the level of satisfaction. Naturally, a follow-up call or contact is important in reestablishing and nourishing the client/customer relationship.

Here are some additional tactics which may work for you:

- **Upgrades:** Everyone loves to be treated to more than what they paid for or expected, be it an airline seat, hotel room, rental car, piece of carpeting, lighting fixtures, etc.
- **Surprises:** We all love them, so why not throw in a few for your customers? It can be anything from a complementary drink to an unexpected gift box.
- **Extra care** ("extraordinary attention"): If you can, go beyond the expected. Carry customers' boxes to the car, do an errand or make a reservation for them, etc.
- **"In their favors":** Bend your policies in favor of the customer whenever possible. Extend the hours, dates, or lower the rates to accommodate their needs. Wave requirements, restrictions, and other artificial rules. They are your rules anyway, not the customers'.
- **Conveniences:** Do whatever you can to make

it more convenient for the customer. Give them a free newspaper or coffee. Better yet, give them breakfast or two dinners for the price of one, etc. Offer 24-hour service, evening hours, or a toll-free phone number.

- **Express services:** While you may not be able to offer everyone a fast or more efficient service level, if you can eliminate the "line" for your VIPs, you will keep them as yours. Pre-authorization, boarding, check-in, etc. are the type of express services which allow your customers to do what they really want today—save time and avoid hassles. The more you can reduce the wait (or better yet, eliminate it) at your point of encounter and provide a hassle-free experience, the more repeat customers you will have for your business.

Whichever tactic you employ, your motivations and justifications are simple—caring for your customers and increasing revenue. Without these, there is no profit.

The third set of tactics which support a strategy group relate to the "post-sell" timeframe. Consider the last few minutes a customer is with you as a window of opportunity allowing you to retain the customer and have them repeat the purchase process in the near future. Here are some post-sell tactics which may help you.

- **The Special Envelope:** Present a note or card to the customer about to depart with a personal note and strong incentive to return. For example, "Dear Mr. Important Irving, it was our honor to serve you. As I know your preference is for the water-view rooms, for your next visit I am reserving the Presidential Suite for you at no extra charge. It also has a lovely water view. We look forward to seeing you soon." Other Special Envelopes can include discounts, upgrades, or complementary items, etc.

- **The Unique Offer:** You can tie the just-completed purchase to the next one through a unique or strong incentive. For example, "Ms. Lost Lucy, if you will return this card the next time you're back in the store, I am going to see that you receive a special matching wallet and key case to the purse you just purchased, absolutely free. They will be reserved in your name. Just ask for me or Ms. Helpful, my manager. That's her signature on the authorization card."

- **The Almost Theres:** An Almost There works similarly to an airline frequent flyer program. It rewards the repeat customer and gives a tangible reward to those who "deserve" one. For example, "Mr. Junior John, I want to thank you for being our customer again. In fact, because this was your third purchase this year, you only have to buy one more and you will receive the fifth one free." You can create almost any Almost There to bring a customer back.

Key points to keeping existing customers:

- Pre-sell reminders and tactics
- Point of encounter delivery beyond the promise
- Post-sell "window of opportunity" return motivators

WINNING NEW CUSTOMERS

More and more, the battle has become one of market share. What can you do to win new customers? How can you attract new buyers? Where will you get more business from this year?

Are there any magical answers? No. However, there are some steps you can take, techniques you can employ, and strategies that work in winning new customers. Winning new customers is usually the result of many steps. Granted, some are fortunate enough to have a new product or service innovation that drives the market to their doorstep. This is the exception. The rule is usually hard work. So let's examine some methods which might help you in the winning of new customers.

Research Do you know where your customers are coming from? Do you know the social-economic status? What about their psychological make-up? The more you know about your existing customer, the more clues you have to locate new ones. Profiling your customers may mean a customer survey, an analysis of addresses, buying demographic data, focus groups, questionnaires, etc. Doing your market research should lead you to the next logical steps: approaches to going after those consumers with similar characteristics who are currently not your customers.

Introductory Offers   Once you have located your new targets, you need to introduce them to your product or services. This simply means almost always having a "special introductory offer." It doesn't have to be a discount; however, it could include a price incentive. It should be a strong enough (or interesting enough) offer to attract someone to want your product or service. What will work for you depends on the market segment, product or service category, etc. In some instances, 50% off, or two-for-ones, are great introductory offers. In other cases, a free gift to first time purchasers is the best incentive. Analyze what has worked for others or in the past for you.

Trial Offers   This is a variation of the introductory offer with a supporting rationale. For example, usually a timeframe is presented to create the perception that action must be taken to gain the benefits of this offer. So, the offer might say, "For the next 30 days. . ." Trial offers can range from special prices to free trials. Trial offers can be limited as to the number of people, i.e., "the first one hundred callers" or to a selected market segment or group. Trial offers can be made for both new and existing products.

Sales   The oldest method of all—and the most frequently used—is simply to have a sale. We all know merchants who have a variety of reasons for a sale in an attempt to attract customers. The reasons for a sale could fill a separate book. Some sales you can have can be tied to the seasons, e.g., "Summer Sale"; holidays, e.g., "Memorial Day Sale"; events, e.g., "Grand Opening Sale"; occasions, e.g., "Birthday Sale"; and the list goes on. Each type of sale attracts or gives your product or service offering another opportunity to win new customers. The key is to have your own tailored calendar of sales.

Tie-Ins Can you develop a tie-in or link with another product or service that gives you a new source of customers? If you have done your research, you will know certain characteristics of your purchasers. Find a match in another service offering and you found a potential new source of customers. Make a joint offer and share a bigger piece of the pie!

Affiliations You may benefit by affiliating with another firm or group of firms to help your brand obtain greater exposure and more awareness with a larger or targeted base of potential new customers. Try to select an affiliation with someone who is larger than you or offers a higher quality image. You will benefit either from the numbers or the image association. Both will help you win new customers.

Associations Involvement by your firm in the right charity, civic, or social entity can bring not only good will, but new customers. For example, I know of one department store which holds an annual sale for the benefit of a special local charity with a part of the proceeds going to the charity. They picked the right group, one with all the wealthy population behind it, and achieve record sales during the event every year.

Strategic Alliances Strategic alliances between nations with a common interest have changed the world—especially recently. Strategic alliances are also occurring more and more between companies in every industry. So why don't you team up with a partner(s) with common interests and start driving in new customers? Don't bother with nonsense networking. Concentrate on who you can really help and who can really help you get business. Make a list of five to ten such groups. Start at the top and get to work.

Uniqueness Look for opportunities to be unique in reaching new customers. Today, you need to break the clutter of offers and stand out from the crowd. One word of caution: don't stand out because of anything that lowers the perception of your product or service. Stand out for reasons which enhance your product or service offering. Look for ways to make your advertising, direct mail, signage, personnel, delivery of service, packaging, and points of encounter to stand out from the competition. Appeal to the senses with color, pattern, design, or whatever works to achieve uniqueness in your product or service category.

The most important step you can take is to develop a "new customer attraction plan" which is your blueprint to building a base of new business from the suggested strategies. Your plan to attract new customers needs to be based on research and contain timetables and expected results from the action steps you develop. Measure each one, and keep and repeat what works.

TAKING CUSTOMERS FROM YOUR COMPETITORS

In our highly competitive world, those who take market share are the victorious. They are also the survivors. To be a survivor requires preparation, knowledge of your competition, and a desire to win. To be victorious requires action plans, based on tactics and strategies that one-up your competitors. Taking market share is an ongoing series of battles. Some are won because of an offensive strategy. Some are lost because of a misguided offense or defensive weakness.

Let's look at some offensive tactics and strategies to take customers from your competitors.

Working Harder   When is your product or service available? Is it more accessible than your competition? Is it accessible when the market wants it? One way to increase revenue and take market share is to extend your hours. Most people would enjoy access to their bank on weekends other than through an automatic teller. Yet most banks are closed. Some have a few hours on Saturday morning in which they are open. When do you really need a bank? Usually on Sunday! Later on we'll look at one bank which works harder by staying open late evenings and open Sunday. It is the market share leader, with 17% of its volume occurring when its competitors are closed! Look at every aspect of your operations to see if you are missing the opportunity to take market share.

Being an early morning person, I am always amazed by one department store chain that opens for business an hour after its competitors in the same location. I watch other early morning people approach the store and simply go to the competition. In fact, most have spent their money and gone home or on to their next stop by the time the store opens. The stores that open an hour earlier are simply taking market share by working harder. Examine your business and look for all possible ways to work harder to take market share.

Work Smarter   Recently, I gave a talk to the customer service department of a large bank in the Midwest. During my talk, I pointed out that while I thought certain aspects of the bank's practices were outstanding, there was one that I couldn't comprehend. For some reason, this bank schedules its ATM (automated transaction machine) maintenance and replenishing between 7:30 and 9:30 a.m. every morning. The bank established this procedure because that is when employees arrive at the various branches—30 minutes prior to opening. The only problem is that between 7:30 and 9:30 a.m. is when most customers need access to the ATM. What do they find? "Out of Service" signs on the machines. Not many people can wait 15 minutes until the machine is serviced, or 30 plus minutes until the bank opens. Having had this experience three out of five times, and observing others experiencing the same inconvenience and frustration, I thought pointing this out to the bank would help. It didn't. So I don't bank there anymore. I use the ATM at another bank right down the street. This bank is just a bit smarter, and they service their ATMs before 6:00 a.m. They view ATMs as one of their primary services to their customers and one which deserves special attention. They work smarter and take market share.

Review your procedures. Were they designed around the traditional work practices or current customers needs? Don't give in to the old way of thinking—that will only lose your market share. One-up your competition by working smarter.

Create Momentum   Ever notice how a crowd gathers? Ever notice where they come from? A crowd gathers because of momentum. People want to be part of a success, event, or where others are going. People don't want to be alone or with the fading entity. Those who are successful at creating a perception of momentum about their brand, product, or service offering can be called "attractors." They first attract interest, and then customers. Where are these new found customers coming from? Where else? From their competition. Masters of creating momentum are masters of taking market share.

Creating momentum requires dynamic action, movement, and excitement. It can be done through public relations, testimonials, staged events, etc. If you wish to take market share, you need to develop your own plan to create momentum. Analyze your competition and determine when and where they are sleeping. Seize the opportunity to create your momentum and take their customers.

The Better Package Is your product or service packaged in line with your target markets? Have you reassessed your look recently? Has your competition changed its packaging? How are they presenting their brand? What do they look like at the point of encounter? Examine everything from their signage to their uniforms. Consider what your consumers will view as better and more attractive.

Brands, products and services fail for many reasons. However, retrospective analysis reveals some common characteristics. These include: not changing at all, changing too late (after the competition has taken market share or the market share has shifted), and not being offensive and going out after the market. If your competitor hasn't changed and isn't demonstrating momentum, you have an opportunity to take away a lot of their clients. You see it happen everyday. Look at Toyota and Lexus and what has happened to the other luxury car competitors who didn't change, repackage, or move with the market. They are trying to regain what may be lost forever. Sony did it in electronics, Disney in entertainment, and Embassy Suites caught the lodging industry sleeping. They built the better mousetrap and created a magnificent, momentum-building campaign to capture market share. Look within your product or service category and look ahead at what you can do to outpackage your competitors. Remember, consumer perception counts as much as reality when going after market share.

Smarter Pricing Packaging and pricing need to work in synergy. How is your competition attracting callers or customers? How does this compare to your offer? You can take market share by simply having the perceived better offer. Your price may be the same (or even more); what matters is how it is expressed. With very few exceptions, people respond to the best perceived price. Value is important in the relationship, but price is what motivates change in behavior in today's marketplace. Here are some examples which may help stimulate your own strategies and tactics with respect to pricing. Think about yourself and your market and which would you call or be attracted to first:

Brand A **Product/Service Pricing**	**Brand B** **Product/Service Pricing**

Special Weekend Rate $49.00 per person
 	
    *   *   *
New York/Los Angeles Fares From $299.00*
*Available 9/15 - 12/15, one way
	$98.00 Sat. or Sun. per room
	
	    * * *
	New York/Los Angeles Fares $598.00* and up
	*Round trip and date restrictions

In the above examples, Brand A and Brand B offer the exact same thing—but the offers are expressed in different ways. What the consumer sees is very different. Given that these companies are in a price-oriented market, it's easy to see that Brand A's phone is going to ring first. If the rest of their service is equal to or superior to Brand B's, they'll come out the clear winner.

What can you do to price and present your product/service offering in its most competitive perspective?

Employee Edge   One of the most powerful forces in the battle to take market share and customers from your competitors is your workforce. Your point-of-encounter employees have both the power of the infantry as well as the ability to wage psychological warfare. Companies that are market share leaders usually have the "employee edge." Their employees are more motivated, more customer-service oriented, and more likely to bring you new customers through providing a good first experience for those who are trial customers. Esprit de corps is something customers feel, notice, and remark about to others. Companies become known for their outstanding employees. This employee edge creates a perception of a winner and generates momentum. This momentum also helps attract the best employees (by being such a good place to work) and new customers (because of the great employees). Momentum leads to market share, because your company stands out from the others.

To achieve the employee edge, you have to begin at home. Supervisors and management often fail to communicate the fact that it is the *customer* who pays the employee as a result of the sale. Look within your own practices to see if you have a reward, recognition or incentive procedure for those whose performance is capturing the customers. If your point-of-encounter employees need something to help them help you, provide it.

How do they look? Like an infantry that is victorious in appearance (one-up on the competition), or like a beleaguered battle group? Point-of-encounter people who look good and feel good about their uniforms and work environment (including employee areas) perform better. If you want the best performers, you have to attract them, train them, and motivate them on to greatness. You also have to be sure that how the customer sees your employees helps give you the competitive advantage.

Recognize that your most valuable asset is the employee who gives your brand the competitive edge by building customer loyalty through their performance. Recognize it and reward it.

Gaining Market Share

- Examine all opportunities to work harder
- Review all procedures to work smarter
- Take the customers' perspective with respect to both of the above.
- Develop a plan to create momentum
- Look at what you can do to outpackage your competition
- Reassess your pricing perception in the marketplace
- Do everything possible to support your employee edge

IV

TECHNIQUES FOR GOOD TIMES AND BAD

GOOD TIMES AND BAD

Customer service is always a form of selling. In good economic times when demand is high, you can maximize profit by "selling-up." "Selling-up" is the term which describes the process of convincing the customer to purchase a higher-priced item, model, etc. When you sell-up, the customer expectation is that you are also going to be providing an even higher level of service. In bad economic times, when demand is low, you can still achieve high profits by maximizing volume through various forms of "selling-down." "Selling-down" is the term which describes the process of convincing the customer to purchase a lower priced item, model, etc. The caution here is that in the service sector, customer expectations may not be lower just because prices drop or extras are added.

Selecting an appropriate service and sales strategy requires focus on the market trends in demand and pricing. You will need to ask several questions: What position does my brand/product/service occupy in terms of the consumers' current perception? Where is my key competition positioned? What type of price/quality service do I want to offer and what strategy should I use? How will my existing customers' perception change if I change my pricing strategy? What strategy will help me attract new customers in view of the current economic/demand forecast? What strategy will help me take market share from my competition?

The following "Demand/Price Strategy Grid" will help answer these questions as well as illustrate some of the selected strategies for selling and service in good times (ref position #1) and bad times (ref. position #9).

Demand/Price Strategy Grid

Price/Demand	High	Med	Low
High	1	2	3
Med	4	5	6
Low	7	8	9

Let's position a brand/product on the grid and discuss strategies related to the economic climate as well as the competitive scenario.

Demand/Price Strategy Grid

Price/Demand	High	Med	Low
High	1 (A)	2	3
Med	4	5	6
Low	7	8	9

In the above scenario, your brand is in position (A), one of the highest priced product/service in a high demand marketplace. The big question is: What direction is the market demand moving? Let's assume demand is going to drop dramatically with a major recession imminent that will last an indefinite period of time. Then demand (d) would be going from high to low. Now you need to go back to your key questions for more answers. You need to ask yourself: Are my competitors likely to enter into a price war with huge discounts? Will anyone take the high road and not discount? How will my customers' expectations and needs be affected by this recession? What will relate to these new needs with respect to my pricing and level of service, etc.?

Once you comprehend where you are positioned on the grid, where the market is going, what will occur with respect to customers' expectations/needs, and what your competition is likely to do, you are almost ready to select both service and sales strategies. Before doing so, you should always ask two more questions. First, as a result of the economic scenario and changing customer expectations/needs, do I now have new or other forms of competition? For example, is telecommunications a new competitor if I am in the travel business? Is shop-at-home service something I am going to have to compete with now? Second, if I change my pricing and/or service strategy, what will my customers and employees think? What do I need to communicate to both? When and how do I do it? In general, tell your employees first or you will have big problems.

We all recognize there is a direct correlation between employee morale and attitudes with economic conditions. Bad times affect just about everyone. So be cautious not to turn your point-of-encounter personnel into a downward spiral with poor communications in such times. We also should recognize (and have our employees do so too) that in bad times, good service attitudes work even better to retain and obtain new customers. Never let your employees confuse a price reduction or sale with an opportunity to reduce service levels. Likewise, even if there is more demand than you can handle, remind all point-of-encounter employees that it is even more critical to provide quality service to avoid losing customers (market share) to your competitors or alternate brands. In essence, service levels should never decrease with pricing nor because of increased demand.

We are now ready to examine some selling and service strategies with respect to good times and bad.

TECHNIQUES AND STRATEGIES

Up-selling   At the points of encounter, be it visual or vocal, up-selling requires developing a technique. Masters of up-selling utilize a variety of techniques, all based on psychological principles to get customers to spend more for what is perceived to be more. These include boasts of having the newest and latest, the longest lasting, the rarest or fanciest, and the attitude that the best costs most. They may also include pitches to ego appeal, prestige associations, and yes, even fear and guilt. Fear and guilt work just great with Lost Lucies and Poor Pauls, especially when they are purchasing for their children.

Now, interestingly enough, up-selling need not be limited to good economic times. A lot depends on the customers' expectations and needs. When to sell-up depends on the customer, competitive strategies, and desired movement in perception for your brand.

Up-selling can work in almost any position on the grid if your product or service is of a quality perception. The approach will vary by customer types, actual product/service offering, and constraints of the competitive environment.

In order to up-sell, point-of-encounter employees need to be trained in "rationalizing" techniques. These techniques help the customer rationalize why they should pay more. For example, a Cautious Carol needs to be told "There is no better line/product. You may be absolutely sure that everyone will be pleased!" An Important Irving needs to hear that there is no finer product than this one.

Up-selling requires careful consideration of your words and visual appearance. For visual appearance—advertising, packages, promotion pieces, displays, and your employees at the point of encounter—take a lesson from the masters: study some of the cosmetic companies. They are masters at perception, up-selling, and point-of-encounter strategies.

Value-Added Selling Providing something extra is the simplest definition of Value-Added Selling. This extra takes many shapes and forms such as extended warranties, extra features or amenities, an additional product, accessories, etc. These must be included at the same price in the order to keep the connotation.

A good value-added item should have a close relationship with the base product or service. The extra must be of a quality similar to your product or service, even if it is an inexpensive item. For example, Career Cathys and Junior Johns generally like to learn about the value-added items, but not at the expense of their request for product detail information. They appreciate the extra when the emphasis is associated with their recognition as a new consumer. Loud Larries love value-added offers which provide another opportunity for them to demonstrate the "deal" they negotiated.

Value-added offers which involve warranty extensions, upgraded items, or additional features work well when the market is in a medium to trading-up mode and with higher pricing strategies (positioning numbers 1, 2 and 4 on the grid). Value-added offers which feature additional product/amenities work well when the market is in the medium demand, trading downward toward low demand positions (numbers 3, 5, and 6), and are especially effective with price offers. The consumer perceives a win/win—reduced price plus value-added tangible.

Point-of-encounter messages in both scenarios need to stress the value-added extra as one more (and major) reason to buy the product or service. Putting a limited time frame on such offers helps enhance the perceived value and create an additional call to action. For someone like a Fast Freddie or Impatient Irene, this "beat the date" concept can be just what makes the purchase. Point-of-encounter employees can close, recognizing the value-added sell is a worthwhile enhancement, which creates a winning message with both existing and new customers. For the existing customer, the message is, "We've added this benefit (extra) in appreciation of your loyalty." For the new customer, the message is, "Try us and you will benefit with this extra—at the same price!"

Try and Keeps We have all heard the adage that "possession is nine-tenths of the law." Well, it may not work that well in sales, but it does work. The concept of Try and Keeps is simply to have the customer experience the product/service and then provide an incentive for him to "keep" it (or in essence, purchase it).

There are a variety of forms of Try and Keeps. These range from simple try-out periods where one can experience the product/service to outright delivery, set-up, and usage of a product for a specified trial period at no cost or a reduced rate. Perhaps one of the best known is the new car test drive. Automobile sales people always want the folks in their showroom behind the wheel. They know how hard it is to resist that new car smell and even harder to resist if you keep the car over the weekend and your neighbors notice!

As you might imagine, Try and Keeps are a disaster if a Returnaround Rhonda responds. On the other hand, a Try and Keep works great with a Slow Sally. Try and Keeps often defuse a Defiant Dan or Threatening Thelma, since the basis for their defiance or threats is removed. The percentage "close" (those who will keep it) on Try and Keeps is particularly good with Cautious Carols, Poor Pauls, Career Cathies, and Junior Johns.

Try and Keeps do best in the strategy/positioning grid when there is movement toward stronger demand combined with economic upturns. This provides a comfort zone where the consumer is trying the product/service and will likely keep it on the basis that "things are getting better." This is also the time to begin moving prices upward prudently. Try and Keeps work well when movement is from medium toward high on the grid (positions number 5 toward number 4, 2, and 1). When movement is trending downward on the grid, the psychological environment for Try and Keeps shifts to a big caution in the consumers' minds. This caution signal says play it conservative— either don't keep it or don't try it now.

Build Selling Designed to build repeat business through an increase in the reward or payoff for multiple purchases, Build Selling works well in times when building customers loyalty is the prime strategy. In terms of the strategy positioning grid, this would be when movement is occurring in either direction from the number 5 position. If there is an extremely high payoff to the customer, Build Selling may also work to take market share in low demand situations. Examples include offers such: as buy just three and get the fourth free; or stay just four nights and the weekend is free; fly six times with us and get a free round-trip ticket, etc. Other forms or techniques of Build Selling include: frequent purchase programs; level of purchase (dollars or numbers) programs; units; price breaks, etc.

Customers who respond best to the Build Selling technique include Fast Freddies, who just love to run up their mileage points, credits or purchases to get that reward fast, Loud Larries who look at achieving the payoff as a means to achieve recognition and attention, Defiant Dans who are looking for the loophole or for you to make a mistake, and, a portion of the Mr. Important

Irvings who believe their multiple purchasing power should be rewarded and receive special attention with a payoff.

Build Selling can be one of the more interesting and positive reinforcers of customer loyalty with point-of-encounter employees. Frequently, customers who respond to Build Selling like or want the same point-of-encounter employee involved with their transaction just to be sure nothing gets lost. In communicating with both your point-of-encounter personnel and your customers, try to avoid changing the rules or program. Such changes, can be perceived as you breaking your promise. Changing the rules mid-stream will bring Defiant Dans and Threatening Thelmas down on you in a trice. No one will feel happy about you removing an award or making it harder to get, especially once they've gotten close to earning it. Point-of-encounter employees will hate to give the bad news to the customers. Build Selling can work well, but it requires consistency and superior communications on all fronts.

Personalized Selling This is the sales approach most closely related to the quality service approach. It is designed to appeal to the individual's desire to be recognized and may also include "ego pleasers" in its scope. In this case, the individual consumer is recognized by name (not number) and, where possible, may even be assigned to one sales or point-of-encounter employee. This technique often requires building a customer history or profile ultimately to provide the service level expected by the customer.

Personalized selling works well at all times and all positions on the strategy grid. One note of caution: with certain customer characters, personalized selling may not be well received when the demand/price strategy is located in the numbers 6–9 grid positions. Examples include Important Irvings who really don't want to be recognized at low-price sales, Career Cathies and Junior Johns whose upward movement takes any downward association into an uncomfortable or perceived backward situation, and to some extent Lost Lucies and Poor Pauls who prefer anonymity as a comfort zone in life. When times are good, personalized/recognition selling works wonders with most people, but especially with Slow Sallies and Important Irvings.

Personalized selling requires procedures and methodology for point of encounter situations. Customer preferences need be recorded and recallable. Name recognition and needs recognition become as important (or more important) than pricing or promotional offers. Personalized matches or napkins, nameplates, monograms, specials cards (VIP plastic) and all other personal recognition are a few examples of personalized selling tools.

Repeats/Come Backs When someone has just purchased, or has had a satisfactory experience with your service offering, they are more likely to respond positively to offers which entice them to return or purchase again. These Repeat/Comeback offers take many shapes and forms, ranging from the simple card offering a special discount with the next purchase, to more elaborate special invitations and promotional offers.

Repeat/Comeback offers provide a dual purpose in that they say "thank you, we appreciate your business," and also provide an incentive to return. The closer to the actual last point of encounter the offer is made, the more likely the success of customer usage. Frankly, these offers work so well, it would be to most businesses' advantage to provide one comeback offer. After all, repeat customers are your least expensive to obtain and most profitable.

It is very difficult for human nature to resist offers such as a complementary dinner on your next visit, an upgrade to a suite or first class seat on your next trip, or a 50% discount on your next purchase. In fact, some customer types are almost guaranteed to respond to such enticements. Characters like Fast Freddie, Loud Larry, Defiant Dan (he just loves to test such offers), and Mr. Important Irving are prime targets.

These Repeat/Comeback offers are most effective when the incentive to return is a strong one. In markets where demand is declining (grid positions number 5, 6, and 8), such offers can maintain market share and customer loyalty and are an excellent defense against price-cutting competition.

Further, the Repeat/Comeback offer, if presented on a personal basis by your service or sales representative, builds a personal relationship at the critical point of encounter. It would not be a rarity to have customers forgive a service flaw because of such offers and the repeat bond that can be built. This personalization approach is particularly effective with Career Cathies and Junior Johns. These individuals respond to the recognition aspect of the repeat offer and begin to build a feeling of comfort with the individual providing the offer.

Switch and Save The concept of a Switch and Save works in selling up as well as selling down. With a Switch and Save, the objective is to take market share, convert consumers to your brand and "switch" customers to purchase a more profitable product or service. There are many forms of Switch and Saves for both selling up and selling down approaches.

When selling up, a Switch and Save can be packaged with a value orientation. For example, "For only a few dollars more, why not have the better model with all the features. In the long run, you will really save." You may imply actual dollars, time, or labor savings.

Another rationale that works well when selling up with a Switch and Save centers on ego and prestige. "Why not switch to this brand? It is much more prestigious and recognized, and now is its only sale so you can really save." In both practice and reality, the item or service switched to actually costs more (the savings in the perceived savings off the non-sale price). Lost Lucies and Poor Pauls are customer characters whose nature is particularly responsive to the up-sell Switch and Save.

The up-sell Switch and Save works very well when movement in the market demand is trending upward (from grid position number 6 toward number 1. When the demand is in a decreasing pattern, a Switch and Save in the form of a sell-down works to retain the customer equally well. Cautious Carols, Fast Freddies, and Impatient Irenes are most responsive to this.

A sell-down Switch and Save is the exact opposite of the sell-up Switch and Save. In the sell-up, your emphasis is on the switch, with save being defined as "a lower price of a more expensive item." In the sell-down Switch and Save, the focus shifts to the word "save." The objective is to retain the customer or achieve a purchase by switching to a less costly product or service which still meets most of the customers' needs. In these circumstances, the following phrases might be heard: "Why not save 25% and purchase this one? It is practically the same." or "Look, you still will be able to have what you really want if we go with the demonstrator at two thousand less." The stronger the Switch and Save in terms of the actual "save," the more likely the customer will purchase, as long as there is some good comparability to their initial wants and needs.

Pay Later/Free For Now   As market demand dwindles in the valley of lowness, the more Pay Later/ Free for Now plans emerge. The concept of Pay Later/Free for Now selling is essentially the same as Try and Keeps. The difference is that Pay Later/Free for Nows are geared toward down times, as this technique allows the consumer actually to take possession or experience the service without paying (until later).

There are many varieties of this form of selling such as: take your vacation now and pay for it with your tax return next spring, or no payments until fall. The rationale and handling of this transaction with your customer is touchy. First, the obvious embarrassment factor (customer has no available cash at the time of desired purchase) needs to be avoided. So, a substitute rationale needs to be suggested by the point-of-encounter employee. This might be expressed as follows: "This is a good deal and they (an intentionally nebulous pronoun) have allowed us to make this special offer that won't tie up your cash" or "I'd take advantage of this no interest charges for 90 days offer." Reasons for handling this type of offer delicately are to keep the customers from thinking there may be something wrong with the deal and changing their minds. Frequently, untrained point-of-encounter employees may lose the sale and the customer by simply saying the wrong words. Examples are, "I know things are tight or uncertain right now, so why not worry about it later," or "You can still avoid the interest charge if you pay in full upon receipt of the first bill." These phrases obviously cause the customer to think versus respond.

Up-Front Selling   When times are really bad, many businesses use Up-Front Selling to stimulate cash flow. To be successful, Up-Front Selling needs to be packaged, usually under the guise of a "substantial savings." Airlines are perhaps the most recognized for Up-Front Selling technique through the "advance purchase" ticket. The discounts associated with such advance purchases form a savings motivation for the customer.

Selling advance purchases in downtrending markets works well with a variety of customer characters. Defiant Dans, Loud Larries, Fast Freddies and Impatient Irenes all like to snap up the bargain and go for it. On the other hand, Lost Lucies, Cautious Carols, and Poor Pauls find it just too complicated or overwhelming—especially when conditions or restrictions are attached to the offers.

Point-of-encounter employees should focus on the substantial savings when communicating with the customer in the pre-sell arena. At the point of actual consumption, the customer, wherever possible, should receive the same treatment as if it were a regular purchase. Also, it is important to state clearly any conditions, especially with respect to refunds or penalties with any advance purchases. Threatening Thelmas and Defiant Dans are just waiting in the wings for you to misrepresent the terms of any up-front sell or advance purchase. When confronted by such customer characters, if you can bend the rules to convenience them, you will convert them to a regular customer. Of course, they will expect you may again allow them to break the rules if they threaten loudly enough.

Down-Selling When your objective is to go for market share in a declining market or you are forced into selling to survive, Down-Selling may work for you. Down-Selling may also be employed at any point on the positioning grid for other reasons such as to encourage trial business, to steal customers from competitors, or simply to get a consumer to purchase. Unlike the various forms of discounting, Down-Selling seeks to either substitute a less costly product or service (one more in line with the customer's perceived expenditure level), or seeks to sell the same product or service in lower demand periods for less.

Down-Selling works well when demand is nearing bottom (positions 3, 6 and 9 on the grid). It also works as a vehicle to move excess inventory. Point-of-encounter employees who are good at Down-Selling focus on the price/value aspects versus the price alone. For example, they may say "This model is a superb value—same brand and quality—just a few less features (some of which you might not want anyway), and at a substantial savings," or "Here is an opportunity to have the same features in a comparable brand for less."

Down-Selling works well with Social Sams, Cautious Carols, Loud Larries, and Fast Freddies. Down-Selling almost never works with Mr. Important Irvings or Returnaround Rhondas. The former views it as degrading and the latter as potentially limiting the game they like to play.

Brand Selling A "brand" is one of the most valuable sales tools you can employ. Just as people have become conditioned to using coupons, so, too, have they learned to look for or respond to brand messages. Interestingly enough, both the use of coupons and the preference for brands cut across almost all market segments. Brand Selling in its simplest dimension is selling your brand versus trying to discount or provide value added services. The sales technique is straightforward: "This is the brand I would recommend," or, "If you're looking for value, you can't beat Smith's."

Selling a brand is selling the "personality" the product or service has established. What brands stand for or the perception consumers have of the brand is the core of a brand's personality. Some brands are the personification of quality. Others are more closely identified with value, and others identified with price. Some brands are "type" brands and others called "designer" brands. The real keys to selling brands are: 1) understanding the direction or mood of the overall marketplace, 2) identifying the type of customer character you are dealing with, and 3) responding with the right message.

In general, brand selling works best at the two ends of the demand/price positioning grid (positions 1, 2, 8, and 9). In the best of times, possessing perceived top quality or "in" brands is almost a national pastime. And, in the worst of times, people tend to look for value, which then takes on a slightly different definition. In low-demand periods, a real value is a brand or known quantity at a sale or discounted price. The real value-seekers respond to a variety of sales messages such as: "This is a once only opportunity to buy Brand X at a substantial percent off," or "You'll never see this price on Brand X again," or "Now you can have the quality of Brand X for the price of one of these unknowns."

Point-of-encounter employees need to focus on Brand Selling as a opportunity to up-sell certain customer characters. Particularly responsive to Brand Selling are Junior Johns, Career Cathies, Lost Lucies, Poor Pauls and Cautious Carols. Interestingly enough, also very vulnerable is Mr. Important Irving. However, here the key to the sale is to offer brand choice, assuming both brands are your most expensive and profitable items.

When using Brand Selling simply to encourage sales in low-demand periods, a comparative sales technique is often employed. The selected brand to be pushed is compared to an unknown of perceived lesser quality which may actually be artificially marked up in price to suggest price parity. Thus, the consumers' perception is that the known commodity—the brand—appears a real value since it is superior to the unknown quantity, but now offered at the same relative price. You have created a comparative choice and stacked the deck for the brand to be purchased. Customer characters who can't resist this approach include Loud Larries, Fast Freddies, and Defiant Dans. Actually, you have a good chance to sell all character types with the exception of Mr. Important Irving. His mentality suggests there must be something slipping in the brand's quality or reputation if it is not more expensive than an unknown.

Other Selling Techniques and Approaches   There are other variations or approaches to selling that can help you win customers in good times or bad. These include:

- *Concept selling*: This is when you're selling a lifestyle or an alternative to the usual, instead of selling an actual production service.
- *Tie-in selling*: This is where you combine your product or service with another in order to create a stronger reason to purchase both goods or services.
- *Co-op selling*: This is similar to tie-in selling except it may not require the purchase of both goods or services. You're simply selling both and either may be purchased.
- *Promotional selling*: This is a form of loss leader offers or introductory offers. There are many more.

The significant point is that regardless of the sales technique employed, for it to be most effective, an understanding of the marketplace, knowing your customers, and training your point-of-encounter employees to appropriately respond must all occur. Likewise, to keep customers and obtain new ones in good times or bad requires these fundamental steps:

- Assess the direction of the market
- Evaluate your competition
- Understand your customer characters
- Select the appropriate sales technique(s)
- Respond with the correct messages or signals
- Train and motivate all point of encounter personnel

Finally, remember, as the market movement occurs, your customer(s) are also dynamic. This means their needs and the signals that relate to these needs shift with the market. While they may not change the core of their customer character, they may well begin to behave and respond more in line with the forces of the marketplace. By using the market demand/price strategy grid, you can plan your responses to be on target with respect to your customers and your competition.

The Up Chart*

Techniques	Best Targets
Up-Selling	Important Irving, Lost Lucy, Cautious Carol, Poor Paul
Value-Added Selling	Career Cathy, Loud Larry, Junior John, Fast Freddie
Build Selling	Fast Freddie, Impatient Irene, Defiant Dan, Important Irving
Personalized Selling	Important Irving, Career Cathy, Junior John, Slow Sally
Repeats/Comebacks	Fast Freddie, Lost Lucy, Defiant Dan, Important Irving, Career Cathy, Cautious Carol, Social Sam
Brand Selling	Junior John, Important Irving, Career Cathy, Lost Lucy, Poor Paul, Cautious Carol

*Demand trending upward with price movement toward numbers 1, 2, and 4 on the positioning grid.

The Down Chart*

Techniques	Best Targets
Value-Added Selling	Loud Larry, Fast Freddie, Impatient Irene, Cautious Carol
Try and Keeps	Slow Sally, Defiant Dan, Threatening Thelma, Cautious Carol
Repeats/Comebacks	Social Sam, Fast Freddie, Defiant Dan, Junior John
Switch and Save	Lost Lucy, Poor Paul, Cautious Carol, Fast Freddie
Pay Later/Free for Now	Fast Freddie, Junior John, Impatient Irene, Social Sam
Up-Front Selling	Defiant Dan, Loud Larry, Fast Freddy, Impatient Irene
Down-Selling	Social Sam, Cautious Carol, Loud Larry, Fast Freddie
Brand Selling	Fast Freddie, Loud Larry, Defiant Dan, Impatient Irene

*Demand trending downward with price movement toward numbers 6, 8, and 9 on the positioning grid.

V

THE ART OF
WINNING

Many firms and organizations strive for quality. They display the awards they've won for service excellence, proudly—but they're prouder of their devotion to quality and the recognition it earns them than of the award. These firms usually are among the more successful in terms of profitability and sales growth.

True, high quality products and top flight service don't guarantee profitability or sales. But, many studies draw correlations between quality and profitability. Some quantitative models suggest there is a theoretical payoff point where the investment in quality peaks maximizes the return on that investment. As you look around the business world you'll see how many companies could easily, and perhaps inexpensively, better their customer service—and thus improve profitability. Comparatively few companies, however, reach or exceed this investment in quality payoff point. Most are willing to settle for lower profits, lower investments, lesser effort. This book is an attempt to reverse that trend—although an excess commitment to quality cannot be recommended either. Obviously it would be great customer service to fly your foreign clients over on the Concorde, but it's the rare commodity that could justify that kind of expense.

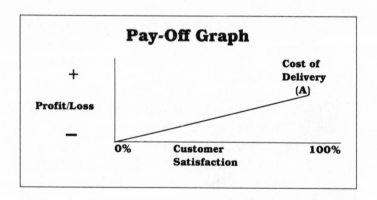

In the graph above, point A, the investment in quality and delivery of such (sales less quality production and marketing costs) is the optimum point at which the greatest return on investment results. Investment to achieve either greater sales or higher levels of service (quality) will cost more than they will potentially return. There are many reasons this phenomenon occurs. These include: 1) the incremental investment causes the price to exceed what the market will bear, 2) the incremental quality achieved is beyond what the market expects (perceives is necessary), and 3) lower cost alternatives become more attractive as a result of greater price differentials. In this graph the dotted line representing cost of delivery is representative only. For your business, the line will probably not be straight or at the same angle level.

Service and Sales Synergy Once you accept the premise that you can overinvest to achieve quality and actually reduce your market, you should be ready to focus on the premise of the need to create a service level and sales strategy that will achieve the highest returns for you. How can you reach Point A previously referenced in the graph for your business? Also, how can you achieve Point A for the consumer?

The consumer views Point A as the "value" point, defined as "quality at a fair price." Assuming marketing and sales have communicated with on-target messages about both the price and quality, the customer should find Point A as the point at which his or her expectations (for both quality and fair price) are best met. When this synergy between the quality (service levels) and sales (marketing messages/price) are achieved, you have the necessary ingredients to add up to a winning formula for success.

In essence, understanding your market needs and responding appropriately are the base steps to developing a customer-retention relationship. Adding the appropriate sales technique will help you close the sale or take market share. Having a quality product or service is only a base ingredient of a more complex formula involving both "internal" (to your own product/service offering) and "external" (to the consumers' needs/types) strategies or focus.

Traditional (Internal Focus)	Contemporary (External Focus)
• Product quality	• Consumer needs
• Cost-drive price	• Cost related to meet needs (expected price)
• Marketing/promotion	• Sales/marketing related customer type
• Distribution	• Communication (between points of encounter and customers)

Who Wins and Why The winners are those who achieve a synergy between the internal and external focus. The winners' actual product quality matches up best to the consumers' needs (internal perspective on target with external focus). The winners produce the quality product or deliver the quality service with prices in line with the customers' expectations. The winners' stated marketing/sales approach relates directly to the customers' rationale (and customer types) for purchasing the product/service. And, at the points of encounter, the product/service delivery allows for the two-way communications process desired by the customer to occur. This latter point is often critical toward achieving total customer satisfaction. The mechanism must exist for dialogue with the customer, for dialogue is considered essential to a quality product/service purchasing experience. This dialogue, or feedback mechanism, is virtually required by many of the customer characters (types) described earlier. It is an integral part of their total purchasing process.

Everything winners do to produce and deliver a quality product or service experience has a common platform—the customer. The greater the focus on the customers' needs, the greater the opportunity to win. This singlemost focus helps set the parameters for quality delivery, price, marketing messages, and point-of-encounter communications. Winners understand the traditional internal fundamentals but do so with their focus on the contemporary external customer marketplace. Winners adjust and respond to the external focus by adapting compatible internal strategies. The resultant synergy produces sales.

Motivating Yourself and Others   Converting winning potential into sales requires going beyond the purely tangible. Those who really win, love. They love life, their jobs, people, helping, *doing*. A company wins when its leaders instill this customer-winning attitude in all employees.

Think of the leaders you consider winners. Isn't this the extra key to their success? Enthusiasm for the job is with customers at all stages of encounter. Management and employees are one group or team. The job is what they are—not where they work. They are a part of the delivery process; they don't witness it, or process people through it.

Winners are involved themselves with the customer. Of course they care about the actual product or service quality production process. But they can participate in this process with the same perspective as a customer. They gain by seeing things from the customer's perspective.

In fact, one of the best of all internal motivators is to accept and implement a point-of-encounter employee's suggestion and let the troops know about it, giving full credit to the member who made the suggestion. Most often, quality delivery improvements come directly from two sources of feedback. The first is from the customer directly, and the second is from the front-line or point-of-encounter employee. Do you have the communications feedback processes in place that allow such suggestions to occur? Moreover, do you have a system set up to credit or, even reward those who make such suggestions?

WINNERS ENJOY THE PERFORMANCE

People who love their job perform. And those who enjoy their efforts become even more motivated to repeat outstanding performance. Their motivation comes from both the tangible rewards of good performance (raises, bonuses, profit sharing, stock, etc.) and from the intangible—from their self-satisfaction at their individual and team's performance.

There are two types of winners. The first win because they do all the measurable things that add up to success. They work hard, avoid mistakes, follow through. Then, there are those who have one more aspect to their character as winners. Their inner motivations may be intangible, but also unmistakable. An excellent company has lots of these people on its staff—because the leaders want it this way, and the employees know that and want to work there. An example of such a company is Disney, where the reputation causes large numbers of applicants from which the self-motivated winners are selected.

THE BEST AT THE ART OF WINNING

The World Institute for Service Excellence recently came out with a recognition list. Every two years, the Institute updates its list based on these eight areas in which an organization must demonstrate excellence:

1. quality product/service delivery;
2. customer relations;
3. employee feedback system(s);
4. employee motivational/incentive performance programs;
5. sales and marketing programs (consumer/ trade);

6. communications to employees and customers;
7. recognition within their respective industry and/or global operating environment by peers and/or other evaluating entities; and
8. having programs/efforts in place for a period of years.

In selecting the cases, multiple factors were taken into consideration. These include:

1. a desire to provide examples with direct employee involvement that demonstrated the promises within this text in terms of dealing with the delivery points of encounter through established programs;
2. cases that demonstrated a relationship between customer recognition and employee motivational programs, resulting in measurable gains in sales or market share;
3. both internal and external "communications" programs which reached their respective targets successfully; and
4. an intentional mix of industries and companies to provide multiple case examples, from global, to national, to regional/local, and from very large to very small in scope.

Special focus was placed on the consumers' perspective in finalizing selections. In essence, these are the "consumers' choice" of organizations which meet their needs the best.

As you look over the list of companies, think about your own experiences as a consumer of these firms' products and services. What have these companies done to win or lose you as a customer? Note how these firms recognize their customers needs, perform to keep these customers, win new customers, take market share, employ different strategies relative to demand, use sales techniques, and become the winners in a highly competitive world marketplace. Millions of consumers have responded positively to their sales and marketing messages. They have retained customers and taken market share with their proven strategies. So look closely at the cases and think about the firms listed. Then, make your own list of what you can do to keep customers and gain market share.

The Top 50 Companies
(Quality Product/Service Delivery and Sales Excellence)

American Airlines
American Automobile
  Association
American Express*
American Hospital
  Supply Company
AMICA Mutual Insur-
  ance Company
Anheuser Busch Com-
  pany, Inc.
AT&T*
Au Bon Pain Company,
  Inc.
Avis*
Banc One Corp.*

Black & Decker Corp-
  oration
British Petroleum
  Company PLC (BP
  America)*
Carlson Companies/
  Radisson*
Coca-Cola
Colgate-Palmolive
Corning, Inc.
Daimler Benz AG
Davis Frame Company*
Delta Air Lines
Deere & Company
Federal Express

Fidelity Investments	Motorola
First National Bank of Chicago	Nestle S.A./Stouffer Hotel Co.*
Four Seasons Hotels	Nissan Motor Company, LTD
GM Cadillac/Buick Division	Singapore Airlines
Grand Met/Pearle, Inc.*	Sony
Harley Davidson	Swiss Air
Hertz	The Limited
H&R Block	Toyota Motor Company/ Lexus*
IBM	
Johnson & Johnson	Turner Broadcasting System/CNN*
John Hancock	
L.L. Bean*	United Parcel Service
Marriott Corporation	USSA
Maritz Companies	Walt Disney Companies
McDonald's	Wells Fargo
3M	Xerox Corporation

*Cases to Follow
Source: The World Institute for Service Excellence

It should be noted there are many other firms that could be recognized for their quality programs, customer/sales efforts and service excellence achievements. Many have been recognized in other works, through the various award programs, and in case studies over the years. The fact of the matter is that quality and service excellence is now a focal point and driving force for many organizations around the globe. More than one or two organizations stand out in virtually every industry. This is a tribute to our improving business society—as both business and government sectors continue to strive for quality. Let's now look at a few extraordinary case examples.

CASE EXAMPLES

The companies profiled here exemplify all the key principles discussed in this text. They stand out in product/service quality, delivery, sales and marketing. They are "customer focused," instead of "self-focused." They recognize the employee as the key asset in keeping customers in good times and bad. They are the best at what they do—the winners.

AMERICAN EXPRESS

American Express has long believed delivery should be the goal of its businesses worldwide. The Chairman of the company also carries the title of Chief Quality Officer to help convey this goal to the entire organization. American Express goes beyond the signals and supports their quality performance with a lot of substance, all focused on one goal—better customer service.

Basic substance begins with superior training (at their "quality university") and full support of senior management. American Express publishes an annual quality management report. Its focus is to emphasize that the corporation is in the customer service business. Employees are routinely expected to go beyond the normal procedures to provide outstanding customer service. Those who do are recognized by a corporate award program.

Like many service organizations, American Express has numerous customer bases to address. The two largest are their cardholders and those who use their worldwide travel services. Necessarily, a lot of time is devoted to see that the relationship between these two provide synergy instead of becoming a source of conflict.

American Express recognizes and practices the steps to customer satisfaction successfully with an immense and diverse group of customers around the globe. It focuses on such customers' needs as timeliness, accuracy, responsiveness, and immediate resolution at the first point of encounter.

Customer satisfaction is constantly monitored and, when new customer needs emerge, new services are implemented to meet these needs. These new services come from one principal source according to company executives, who at the first International Quality Service Summit stated, "Virtually every new service introduced by American Express during the past ten years came directly from the suggestions and expressed needs of the customers themselves." In addition to listening to their customers, American Express employees are asked to spend 10% of their time striving to improve their job of delivery service. The result is many internal and procedural changes resulting ultimately in better service to the customers.

American Express sincerely believes that the key to success begins with not only pride and motivation of the employees, but with ongoing research into both job enhancement and customer-needs identification. It utilizes sophisticated research techniques and the latest technology to quantitatively and qualitatively assess the needs of the customer. From these assessments delivery of service improvements and new services are developed for its card membership. Ultimately, American Express wants its customers to feel that it is the only company they want to do business with.

To sell consumers on American Express requires a multifaceted marketing approach. For the end user (actual cardholders and prospective new cardholders), American Express has employed an arsenal of marketing messages and weaponry. Advertising has imprinted messages such as "Don't leave home without it!" in just about every American's memory bank. More messages associated with service, reliability, prestige, and acceptability are directed at the end user as both retention and trial marketing mechanisms. Its marketing messages address the conscious and subconscious needs of virtually every market segment. Regardless of the promotional or sell strength, the image is constantly reinforced—an image of quality, competence and service excellence on an array of services. You can probably recall the television commercial showing a world traveler receiving his prescription by calling American Express's global assistance line.

American Express deals with virtually every customer character type on earth, yet there are certain common elements to their success formula. These include getting employees involved to better their jobs so they can better service the customer; a passion for listening to the customers' needs and responding with action and implementation of new services promptly; addressing the needs of service consumers promptly, accurately and with dependability around the globe with targeted marketing messages; reinforcing their quality image in how they promote and market their brand; and having the basic quality systems fully operating and in place at all customer contact points.

I would be remiss if I didn't emphasize some of the innovative services introduced year after by the industry leader—things we now take for granted—because American Express is there doing it for us. Things like: cash when and where we need it; replacement of lost travelers checks (not to mention the checks themselves); global assist programs which help their card members with virtually any need, anywhere on earth; Gold cardholder account statements and categorizations at year end that make preparing your tax returns comparatively easy; a product/service guarantee program that makes returns simple and workable (Returnaround Rhondas love you, American Express); very high credit (the Mr. Important Irvings perceive this credit as virtually limitless); translation services; lost luggage assistance; and the list could go on for pages.

In essence, American Express quality service levels

and innovative new service offerings have improved an entire industry as competitors strive to keep up with the leader. Leadership, quality service, customer satisfaction, and marketing are what make American Express a winner and in the category of the very best at service and sales excellence. "Membership has its privileges!"

AT&T

Until the breakup of AT&T, most consumers didn't view Ma Bell as providing a service, or for that matter, services. People take for granted those daily conveniences that are actually quality services until they experience disruption, change, or alternatives. Such is the case of AT&T. Be it the pace of technological change, the vastness of the AT&T service spectrum and innovative marketing, or comparison with its new competition, finally AT&T is now being recognized as a quality service provider. Let's examine how AT&T retains market share, keeps existing customers and adds new ones after a period when multiple competitors made inroads in the marketplace.

First, one must recognize AT&T is a very well managed, well run corporate entity—not a bureaucracy, but a business. Its leadership is dedicated to quality service excellence and its senior management expert at marketing and product development. AT&T, perhaps more than any other organization on earth, deals with, and must understand, the needs of all customer character types, individual market segments, commercial market segments, and multi-national entities. In all cases, AT&T's focus is on customer needs and service.

Second, AT&T lives with, practices, implements, and causes change in the marketplace. It is proactive at bringing customer needs and new services together. It is innovative with its product, service offerings, pricing, and marketing. AT&T is all these things because each is addressed with a formal plan, extensive product and service research and development, consumer market research and feedback systems, and an investment in training its people.

Third, AT&T is a master at one of its own businesses—communications with the marketplace through direct sales, mail, promotion, advertising, and marketing. It communicates its technological accomplishments in the form of new services and, in doing so, is constantly reminding the marketplace how it is acting to meet their needs.

Fourth, it recognizes virtually every market segment and its needs. For example, to its corporate customer, AT&T sends messages emphasizing their reliability and technological superiority. For others, such as the emerging new customer (Junior Johns, Career Cathies, etc.), they emphasize their overall value and acceptance. To others, the message may be price, and to still others, capabilities.

Fifth, it focuses on providing solutions to consumer problems. It brings its immense resources to play for individual problem resolution. AT&T thinks like the best and acts accordingly.

Here are just a few of the innovative and on-target service offerings introduced by AT&T.

- Call Waiting
- Call Forwarding
- Conference Calling
- Direct Dial International Service
- Language Line
- 800 Number Service
- Combined Phone and Credit Card
- State-of-the-Art Switching
- Monitoring

Think about the value of just some of these services on a practical everyday level. Think of the child calling home with her last coin in need of help and her ability to get through to her parents because of call waiting. Think of the farmer or rancher or forester who injures himself and can reach help with a modular portable phone. Think of the news reporter in the middle of a global crisis who went to an AT&T phone and broadcast on-the-spot coverage of events as they occurred. The combined phone card and credit card was an enormous success, far outstripping experts' predictions. AT&T waived forever the yearly fee for customers who signed up in the first year of offering—a risky Try and Keep offer, instead of the usual Pay Later/Free for Now offer used by many credit card offering companies which waive the fee only the first year for new customers. Result: AT&T grabbed significant market share.

Each of these examples show a company not

only meeting needs, but improving their customers' daily lives—perhaps even saving them!

At the First International Quality Summit, co-sponsored by AT&T, Randall Tobias, AT&T's Vice Chairman, stated: "While customers are noticing improvements, we must improve more and faster to continue exceeding their expectations." He went on to state that "When there is technological parity, the market share game will be won by those who are more responsive to the customer. . . . Customer service will become the critical factor in market differentiation."

To achieve a quality service offering, AT&T utilizes a simple yet powerful organizational philosophy which essentially turns the traditional organization chart upside-down, making the point-of-encounter employees appear at the top and top management at the bottom. The role of all those below the customer-contact employee is to provide resources and help to achieve quality service and customer satisfaction. This includes the chairman, senior management, technicians, research and development—everyone to support the efforts of the point of encounter employees.

Employee motivation, training, customer feedback mechanisms, empowerment, removal of internal roadblocks, clear communications, employee feedback, and quality improvement teams are all standard processes at AT&T. It is with these tools and practices that AT&T is able to carry out its quality goals and objectives to be perceived one of the very best at quality service.

AVIS

Avis provides an ideal example of a firm where the employee plays the key role in all aspects of the product/service offering. When Avis formed an ESOP (Employee Stock Ownership Plan), they gave their employees a share in the ownership of the company. Thus, their employees have the ultimate motivation. They own the company, so they do "try harder."

Avis also established a program called "EPGs" which stands for "employee participation groups." The EPGs are charged with providing a flow of information through all levels of the organization. The information contains improvement suggestions, efficiency and cost concepts. The meetings are held monthly at over 80 locations. Further, regional reviews are scheduled quarterly and a two-day meeting with the company's chairman and CEO, Joseph Vittoria, and senior management is conducted annually. Many of Avis' service and work process innovations have resulted from the EPG process.

Avis' senior management is "field active"— constantly visible and fostering the team concept. A comprehensive communications program keeps all employees informed, motivated, and customer-oriented.

Here are two examples of how employees seek to improve costs and better serve the customer:

Employees, through their EPG, developed a totally new car check-in system. The "toll plaza" concept allows the customer to be checked-out without going to a counter or waiting in long lines. I remember being caught at the Miami airport in a torrential tropical downpour. Avis efficiently prepared my bill while I sat comfortable, cool, and dry, I remained in the car. I got my receipt and made it to the plane faster than I expected.

At another location, someone suggested adding the color of the car to the identification information provided the customer upon receiving the rental agreement. This simple, practical suggestion helped many locate their cars quickly in lots where the bus driver wasn't allowed to do so for the customer.

Avis also has demonstrated the use of technological innovation and advances aimed directly at improving customer service. Its Wizard reservations system is constantly improved to provide agents up-to-date information on its customers. The rapid check-in process utilizing agents in the lot with hand-held transmitter/computer/printers provides every demanding Fast Freddie customer a statement before they can put their coats on and grab their briefcases.

Marketing and operations, employees and management, all move in the same direction with the same goals and motivation: to meet the customer's needs. The rewards and motivation: *shared* profits.

BANC ONE

Recently, *The New York Times* called Banc One "The Best Little Bank in America" and only a week earlier, *Institutional Investor* ran a cover story entitled, "The Magnificent McCoys. Running America's Best Bank." Banc One Chairman, John B. McCoy, and his bank corporation continue to flourish and grow in a burdened and troubled industry. Banc One banks continue to keep existing customers and add new ones of every customer type. How does a really not-so-little bank (recently moving into the top twenty in size) win customers and retain their favor? How does Banc One counter one of the strongest downtrend periods of any industry? Why do its customers not only have faith in Banc One, but are among the most loyal of any service industry brand?

For our purpose, we will exclude Banc One's brilliant financial strategies and concentrate on the plethora of customer and employee-related endeavors. Their current advertising theme, "Whatever It Takes," is the capstone of their whole program.

John B. McCoy believes "the game in the 1990's is market share." The chief way they have been able to make huge advances in market share has been by making themselves customer favorites. The Banc One branch nearest me is open from 9:00 a.m. to 7:00 p.m. weekdays, 9:00 a.m. to 5:00 p.m. on Saturday, and even noon to 5:00 p.m. on Sunday! They hold sidewalk sales and grill hot dogs and hamburgers. New branch banks feature glass atriums, comfortable seating areas and fresh coffee. Add to these winning employee attitudes and the fact that they offer an extra one-quarter percent attitudes interest on six month CDs, and you can see why they are leading their 18 competitors.

Like most successful businesses, Banc One reinvests a share of its profits to make itself and employees even better. For example, three percent of its profits every year go into research and development—often aimed at improving customer service. It continues the customer and quality focus right down to the performance evaluation process in which at least half of the merit raise is directly tied to "quality objectives." Top performers are recognized by the company chairman on a personal basis for achieving their objectives.

Charles Aubrey, Vice President and Chief Quality Officer, has devised a comprehensive system which appraises the value of the Banc One's quality strategies. He credits quality management with contributing $6–7 million to bottom line profits. Strategies include: quality audits, customer satisfaction surveys, measuring retention rates, and valuing of new business. Quality teams solve problems as well as launch new opportunities. Branch offices are continually monitored and assessed with over a quarter of a million customer satisfaction surveys, as well as use of covert shoppers who even count the smiles per point-of-encounter employee.

Training and guidance help to keep these efforts a top priority. A new program called "Quality Champions" has covert shoppers spend time training staff on how to improve the quality of their service.

To the customer, Banc One's message is straightforward—"Whatever It Takes" to meet your needs, to keep you as a customer, or to win you over as a new customer. The W.I.T. program awards point-of-encounter employees with a special button called a "Witty" to those observed doing the job in the true spirit of the slogan. The criteria are superior work or effort exceeding the normal boundaries, an extra effort which results in retaining a customer, an effort requiring significant sacrifice of personal time or resources in order to do "Whatever It Takes," and an effort which encouraged or resulted in superior teamwork. In essence, every Banc One employee shares the same three-word job description—"Whatever It Takes."

BRITISH PETROLEUM COMPANY PLC/BP AMERICA

BP America managed a magnificent image change during its conversion of Sohio stations. Think about a company in a highly patriotic time (during the Gulf War) in a fiercely patriotic area - the Midwest, changing its look from red, white and blue to green and yellow. No small task. Why BP did it and how they achieved it is worthy of a case history in any book dealing with the customer, image, and marketing.

The Sohio brand was established and a traditional leader in the marketplace. However, it was getting old in the look of the stations and stores. People perceived Sohio as belonging to a local market instead of as nationwide or global brand. Customers thought of Sohio as 1970s-style gas stations, not 1990s-style auto care facilities plus convenience stores.

After acquiring Sohio, BP successfully repositioned it with a well-chosen name selection ("BP America") and excellent consumer-oriented marketing steps. Today, many consumers in the local market feel BP America is as American as was Sohio. How did a company originally named British Petroleum achieve this? It's a story of extraordinary community relations and communications with all constituencies.

BP's leadership made some very smart decisions. First, they not only kept Sohio's headquarters in Cleveland, Ohio they built a landmark office tower which became the pride of the city. Second, the top management of BP America, as well as its parent in the UK, communicated openly and effectively with the local community about its investment in the area. Third, BP America was recognizably generous and active as a good corporate citizen. In fact, BP America ranked number one in its philanthropic givings to the community. In essence, management was smart, sensitive, and on target with its posture to the home community. They probably would have fallen significantly short had they not undertaken all of the above steps.

With their corporate image and community relations plan in effect and working, BP America
embarked on a classic, complete "new look and
feel" updating of its physical facilities and product
lines. The old red, white and blue motif was
changed with an astonishing pace and effectiveness.
Contemporary back-lighted plexiglas in bright green
with yellow letters coated every facility. Silver,
smooth-flowing covers for gas pumps and other
station facilities added to a year 2000 look. New
doors, glass, paint, pavement, pumps, landscaping, uniforms, merchandising displays became
ubiquitous overnight. The new look appeared on
signs, gas stations, convenience center islands,
BP Pro-Care Service Centers, car washes, etc.
Employees received new uniforms, pencils, pens,
pads, and a tremendous amount of motivation
and communications.

BP America recognized that to execute such a
massive change its task force would have to look
beyond themselves and keep the customer informed and responding. It did so by employing a
complete array of marketing techniques, promotional offers, timely public relations and measured
communications. As a consumer, you saw the
changes and were aware of it, but never once did
BP America ask you to think about it.

Some competitors tried to cause a negative feeling by advertising they were still "red, white and
blue, 100% American"—a direct shot at BP and its
color change. BP took the high road with quiet
speed and strong consumer promotions to encour-

age new trial experience as well as reward existing customers. Free dollar-off coupons, free car wash coupons, free oil and lube certificates, and free soft drinks all drew existing customers and new customers to see the changes.

And what they saw, they loved. Clean and new gas stations. Employees in fresh new uniforms with smiles and enthusiasm. More convenience, offers, and benefits directly related to the needs of the market. These combined with massive public relations stories on the corporation's investment in the local community, its sponsorships of weekend and even week long events, its charitable giving leadership and participative executives in community renewal led to an overwhelmingly positive reception. People felt positively toward the company, its product and service offerings and its employees.

BP understands what motivates brand loyalty in its marketplace. It understands the value of involvement, change, and marketing. The results have been extraordinary goodwill, customer retention, new trial business, and improving in a market where traditional logic would lead one to conclude it wouldn't have been possible.

CARLSON COMPANIES/RADISSON

The Radisson Hotel Corporation, part of Carlson Companies, developed a customer service training program called "Yes I Can." The goal of this program is to anticipate the needs and the expectations of their guests and exceed these. The program is aimed at all point-of-encounter employees and includes a comprehensive general employee training section, a department-specific training component, and systematic follow-up procedural program.

Radisson President, John Norlander, notes: "the program directly addresses the company's mission statement to develop and implement strategies that exceed the expectations of three constituents—owners/developers, guests, and employees." In a highly competitive industry, focus on assets productivity is imperative.

During general employee training, employees from different departments in the hotel come together to focus on why guest service is important, discuss service situations from a customer's point of view, and are then inculcated in Radisson's Guest Service standards.

Next, each department supervisor conducts department-specific training with their staff. Using the Radisson Service Assessment, employees evaluate the quality of service in employee/guest situations against Radisson's guest service standards. They also practice applying the four "Yes I Can" key service skills and meeting service standards in tough service situations. These key service promises are: 1) meet and exceed guest expectations, 2) communicate effectively, 3) work as a team, and 4) handle difficult situations effectively.

The follow-up program is a series of one hour monthly departmental meetings where Radisson's service standards are further defined for each specific department. These sessions also involve employees in goal setting and action planning to improve the department's weak areas of service. Star performers are rewarded.

A "Yes I Can" team is made up of a selected group of line employees who represent all departments in the hotel. A manager works with the team, on a monthly basis, to increase communication and understanding between departments and to suggest and help implement strategies for resolving problems and improving quality service. Employee newsletters, employee bulletin boards, lunches for "Yes I Can" star performers and other motivational and communications vehicles are used on a regular basis to reinforce the program.

The key to the "Yes I Can" program is the Management Training provided to all department heads and supervisors so they not only understand how to implement the program, but also comprehend the vital role they play in keeping the "Yes I Can" attitude alive.

Managers are asked to model the Radisson Standards of service by treating employees in the same manner that the "Yes I Can" program asks employees to treat their guests. They are also taught how to recognize and support the actions of the employees who make "Yes I Can" guest service decisions—even when the service situation could have been handled differently. Whether the action was right or wrong, it is important supervisors reinforce the fact that the employee was acting on the guest's behalf. Techniques are covered on how to respectfully coach employees to improve their guest service skills, and all hotel management staffs are asked to examine policies and procedures to ensure that they do not hinder the employees' ability to give "Yes I Can" service.

Radisson's customer service program supports the synergy between sales and service. The "Yes I Can" philosophy makes it clear that it is the job of every employee to create and keep customers. As Sue Gordon, Vice President of Human Resources, states: "We could even go as far as to say that the slogan alone empowers a Radisson line employee." It pushes the responsibility and authority to handle customer service situations down. If Radisson is asking them to say "Yes I Can," then Radisson is asking *them* to handle the situation to the best of their ability. The program communicates the concept that each employee within the hotel, whether they work in the front or the heart of the hotel, has endless opportunities within each day to influence a guest to return or not to return. Marketing and sales generate trial business, but it is the positive service experience of the guest that ensures repeat business. Employees begin to recognize that in reality, there is no distinction between sales and service—sales is a part of service, if only by the act of delivering golden moments of truth and realizing return guests and word of mouth referrals.

The direct results of the "Yes I Can" program are evidenced in many locations throughout the country. In a period when the overall lodging market was in recession, Radisson Hotels showed gains in market share directly attributable to a very high repeat business.

In guest surveys, repeat visitors were asked why they elected to return to the same hotel. The results strongly indicated because of the positive "Yes I Can" attitude of the hotel staff. In a highly competitive marketplace, this customer service program made a tangible difference to individual hotel performance. It also provided a positive impact on all other Radisson Hotels in the chain.

THE DAVIS FRAME COMPANY

The Davis Frame Company in Brownsville, Vermont is, in essence, what others wish they could be—the best by intent, design and personalization.

After working with timber frame companies for more than a decade, master craftsman Jeff Davis and custom builder Rick Bascomb formed the Davis Frame Company with a simple objective: "to build the best post and beam homes by handcrafting each post and beam to perfection." To achieve this objective, The Davis Frame Company takes some extraordinary steps and does some unique things.

The company employs craftsmen and artisans whose ancestors taught them unique skills such as expert timber cutters, finishers and joiners who carefully handcraft each post and beam. Not only do they have the best employees, they give those employees the best materials to work with. New England has some magnificent forests, but Jeff Davis goes to Oregon to procure the finest grade Douglas Fir, straight grain, minimal knots, light in weight, and as strong as oak for the frames. He has the lumber trucked to his craftsmen in Vermont where each piece is then hand-cut, planed, chamfered, and sealed. Why does Davis transport timber across the country when it is readily available literally in his back yard? Passion. Davis has a passion for quality that only true craftspeople can understand.

Every home is designed together with the owners to meet their desires and reflect their personalities. Each house, therefore, has a unique character which ensures that no two will ever be the same. Each home bears the name of the family who jointly designed it with the firm. The Davis Frame Company then does not produce "a colonial" or "a contemporary", it creates "the Ricci home" or "the Fricke home." As Jeff Davis states, "Tucked away in the back of one's mind is a vision of their ideal home. Our goal is to make that vision a reality."

His marketing and sales process totally integrates the customer and seller into a single team, moving toward the common objective of total customer satisfaction. Early on, Davis invites prospective customers to inspect and visit other homes he has built, talk with owners, and meet the craftsmen. The firm works with the customer from site selection to landscaping. The Davis team stays with the customer every step of the way. They invite the customer to join them when the timbers are selected, when the timbers arrive for finishing in Vermont; they suggest tone, grain, or any other appearance changes on site or anywhere along the process. And naturally, if anything needs to be changed, even after the home is completed, the team takes care of it.

The Davis Frame company epitomizes personalized customer service, quality, employee involvement, uniqueness and excellence in marketing and sales. It is an example everyone from employee to owner can learn and benefit from. Think about those things we strive for such as pride, understanding your customer's needs, motivation, fulfilling expectations, targeted and on-target marketing, sales techniques, packaging and merchandising approaches, customer feedback, and an obsession with quality and being the best. Naturally, word of mouth and customer testimonials are strengths in the sales and marketing strategy, but so too are involvement of the customer themselves, flexibility, openness and need fulfillment. The Davis Frame Company experienced a record year in 1991, at the height of the recession and in the middle of a depressed housing market. They prove market and financial performance can be achieved in bad times as well as good for those who understand the customer's needs.

GRAND MET/PEARLE, INC.

The world's largest optical retailer of eyeware and eyecare products understands they cannot survive without continued customer satisfaction. On the other hand, if Pearle satisfies its youngest customer, they can remain a customer for life. To do so, Pearle invests heavily in an extensive customer tracking system called the PRO System. This system updates customer records and keeps track of inventories. After all, having what the customer wants in stock or at the point of encounter is essential in a business where the total decision may occur spontaneously and the transaction takes less than an hour.

Pearle provides its point-of-encounter employees multiple seminars and training courses on such subjects as service excellence and effective sales techniques. The Pearle Eyecare University programs are highly regarded by its industry. In addition to their training, Pearle has an extensive quality-assurance program. Lenses must pass multiple accuracy tests and checks before reaching the customer. Pearle conducts field audits on a regular basis, including equipment inspections and employee evaluations. An extensive list of company quality and customer service standards must be met.

Pearle is the market share leader as well as the quality leader in a highly competitive field. One reason why is because they aggressively market themselves. In addition to a successful advertising campaign, they have developed a calendar of promotional offers to keep existing customers and win new ones. They must employ multiple marketing techniques, ranging from two-for-one sales to up-selling. Their innovative Pearle Express service is exactly what Fast Freddie and Impatient Irene asked for! And, their quality assurance professionalism is soothing to the Cautious Carols and Poor Pauls of this world.

An exemplary training program they offer is called "The Profitable Art of Service Recovery." This unique program recognizes that mistakes can occur, and provides a blueprint for point-of-encounter employees to overcome the mistakes and retain the customer. The program provides techniques to overcome adversities and centers on adopting a customer-focused attitude that empowers point-of-encounter employees to act to recover the customer. It further provides an economic perspective for the employee that ties customer satisfaction to revenue generation.

Pearle's sales approach emphasizes point-of-purchase merchandising that also represents its quality image. Its locations feature pop-up displays, poster, stanchions and color photo offers, all displayed tastefully and offering good values. Its employees are trained to provide answers, service and fulfillment of the in-store offer. This in-house store merchandising is an opportunity often missed by quality-oriented firms who think an empty store or a lack of sales promotional materials means a quality look. Not only do some miss some revenue-generating opportunities, they miss the consumer's need perhaps to purchase more or desire additional products or service.

Grand Met, Pearle's parent company, extends a philanthropic philosophy of doing something for the community it services through a variety of charitable endeavors, including providing eyecare for many who can't afford it. All of these factors help keep Pearle a winner where it counts—with the customer—of all ages and types.

L.L. BEAN

L.L. Bean has been a pioneer of customer service. It began offering its customers a 100% satisfaction guarantee in 1912. It still does today. The current L.L. Bean is a model of point-of-encounter experiences and appearances meticulously orchestrated to provide a harmonious experience for the customer, whether the sale occurs in their Freeport, Maine store, over the 800 phone number, or through a catalog purchase. L.L. Bean is also a model of sophisticated consumer research at work, analyzing, experimenting, collecting data, and constantly applying research findings to enhance its offers to the consumer.

Start with the store: it says "quality" with one look. The clean, directional signage, well-landscaped entry with brick stairs and walkways, and green signage and white facility look inviting from the outside. (The catalog and mailings also appeal visually to the customers' expectations, regardless of character type or market segment.) The traffic flow at the entry is a composite of value and quality seekers from every market segment, age bracket and every corner of the globe. Upon entering, the extensive use of wood, light effects, and constantly rotating merchandise displays create an instant warmth. Immediately visible are customer opinion forms, order forms, store directories, and helpful personnel. As soon as you walk in, you know you are in a special store. The feel is a comfortable— even with a plethora of shoppers around you.

L.L. Bean offers unusual quality merchandise in wide selection and ample supply. Pick up a pair of slacks, and you'll try them on in a meticulously clean fitting room with help standing by in case you'd like them hemmed while you wait by one of the on-premises tailors. That is what customer service is all about.

The employees form a visual extension of the L.L. Bean quality dressed in the green and white theme or contrasting khaki brown. They are as adept at handling Impatient Irene as they are Social Sam. Spotting signs that a customer is on vacation draws a "May I ship these back home for you?"—a much more pleasing sentence than "We only take MasterCard or VISA."

Before that extra sturdy, extra large, high quality L.L. Bean shopping bag (with green letters on white background) gets too heavy, an employee offers to hold it for you while you finish shopping. You notice your eyes have improved because you can not only find the tags, you can read them— large letters or type? If an item in the display doesn't feature your size or color, an employee is ready to bring it out to you right then and there or, if it's not in the store's inventory, they offer to send it to your home.

As you no doubt are aware, the quality of the merchandise is all top quality. Naturally, returns and exchanges are no questions asked. L.L. Bean attends to customers 24 hours a day—for that is their policy—"We're always open."

While every inquiry, even those of an Important Irving or Junior John, is responded to with competence, you will notice just how sophisticated the business management side of high technology is working. For example, there is an ongoing restocking process to assure incoming merchandise arrives on the store floor promptly and constantly, and that the last busload of shoppers' destruction of the neatly stacked piles of merchandise lasts only a few moments. Cash register personnel always check that customers have the latest catalog or are on the mailing list.

L.L. Bean puts it all together—both doing their homework on what the customer wants and needs are, as well as how to fulfill those needs in every way. They succeed because they are masters at both point-of-encounter marketing as well as at direct mail sophistication. L.L. Bean prepares state of the art customer history and profiles from its own data research and from secondary sources such as credit card data bases and list profiles. Its offers, while highly targeted, are also always in keeping with the quality service and sales excellence standards it has set and the customer has come to expect.

Does it work? L.L. Bean has one of the most loyal customer bases of any business in the world. Its repeat factors are very high and customer satisfaction ratings are at the top of not only retailers, but almost all businesses. Moreover, it works to perpetuate itself through extensive word of mouth. Loud Mouth Larries can be found in every city willing to bend your ear about L.L. Bean. Even an Important Irving won't hesitate to reveal his gear which came from L.L. Bean. L.L. Bean is big business at its best—being small and personal to the customer.

STOUFFER HOTEL COMPANY

Selected by the Harvard Graduate School of Business as a service industry case study example, the Stouffer Hotel Company exemplifies its parent company Nestles' philosophy of offering "only the very best" in quality service. Virtually unknown with consumers in the mid-80's in its industry, the Stouffer Hotel Company has developed into a quality leader in its industry and gained the reputation as a major player in the marketplace. It has achieved its recognition as a result of a number of specific strategies.

First, the company has been very careful in its site location. An important factor is that it has insisted on owning and managing all the hotels and resorts that bear its name. In an industry that is highly franchised, this has allowed for product and service level consistencies. By owning and managing all of its hotels and resorts, Stouffer's ensures their quests enjoy a consistent level of service. Stouffer's also distinguishes itself by not segmenting its brand (putting the same name on different quality and service level lodging facilities), which means guests can expect the same level of comfort and service at all locations.

Stouffer's offers numerous consumer-oriented services, many of which they were the first to introduce. These include: complimentary coffee and newspaper delivered to the guest's door at the time of their wake-up call; complimentary shoeshine service; free in-bound FAX and/or cost-fixed outbound FAX charges; clear telephone policies, including no exorbitant surcharges; complimentary airport pick-up and drop-off service; and express check-in and check-out. To its partners in travel, Stouffer's offers the travel agent community one of the fastest commission payment time frames in the industry (within 48 hours), an annual "Room-on-the-House" program (use of rooms free to travel agents during specified time-frames), and other innovative incentive programs.

Stouffer hotel-level employees, from the van drivers to the bellmen to the room service personnel, go out of their way to help guests. The friendly and professional attitude of the employees helps Stouffer's stand out in a very crowded upper tier of the lodging pyramid. The professionalism is constantly reinforced through comprehensive training programs at all levels of the organization.

Employee motivation, communications and training systems are an integral part of the Stouffer Hotel Company management system. All point-of-encounter employees are regularly reminded of customers' needs through training programs. Also, every sales related person undergoes an equally comprehensive customer and sales training program called the B.E.S.T. program (Building Effective Sales Techniques). To be sure all understand the importance of these programs, senior management participates both as students as well as teachers throughout the year.

Intercompany communications include newsletters, video tapes, "Marketingrams," personal visits, etc. Motivational performance awards available to employees at every level are the center of attraction at annual meetings. Winners get put up in suites and are publicly praised.

Consumer feedback systems include Stouffer's Guest Relations Program, honored as the best in the industry by the American Hotel and Motel Association. Guests may use a red phone in the lobby to speak directly to the hotel general manager to resolve problems on the spot. Customers are encouraged to fill out a questionnaire which results in a qualitative and quantitative score card for each hotel, and a compensation system which directly ties to the consumer rating for management and employees. Additionally, senior management is directly involved with the customer on a regular, ongoing basis, be it the individual traveler with a problem, the professional travel agent, the corporate meeting planner, or other traveling executives. They are not allowed to work in an ivory tower, leaving all customer contacts to the rest of the staff.

Stouffer's takes care that their marketing is in tune with the customers' needs and expectations. They have consistently been recognized for their leadership in the marketing area by offering an ongoing array of consumer benefit promotions.

The Club Express program provides frequent guests with an array of extraordinary service benefits—things like upgrade to the Club Floor rooms, club lounges complete with snacks and beverages; concierge services; etc. In addition, their repeat visits are rewarded with their choice of travel-related gifts; American Express gift checks, U.S. Savings Bonds and other items.

The Share Across America/U.S. Savings Bond program has been so well received by consumers that Stouffer's is the single largest provider of U.S. Savings bonds to the public after only the U.S. Treasury, banks and the armed forces. In fact, Stouffer's efforts here earned them the first Kate Smith Award given by the Treasury for promotion of investment in Savings Bonds.

Other consumer marketing concepts—such as sponsoring the weather in *USA Today, Wall Street Journal* and on the Weather Channel—provide consumers with yet another reason to feel good about the Stouffer brand. Supporting major local charities with their hotel openings, and providing secretaries incentives to book Stouffer rooms are still more examples of this winning strategy.

Stouffer Hotels lives up to the goal of its parent, Nestle S.A. to be the very best in its service category.

TOYOTA MOTOR COMPANY/LEXUS

When Toyota Motor Company introduced the Lexus, they did so in an extraordinary manner. Toyota at first knew they had a problem. They recognized that in the United States market and others they did not have a reputation for building larger cars, luxury cars, or cars in a high price range. But they knew they had one thing going for them: the Toyota car brand was widely associated with value and quality. Clearly, they had to take that reputation and convince customers they could deliver on a whole new type of product.

To begin with, Toyota spent countless hours on consumer market research. The results allowed them to conclude which specific steps they would need to take to break into this new market of upscale automobile owners and leasees.

Research said what people disliked most was the auto service establishment (the dealership) and related servicing. Research also said people don't strongly associate the name Lexus with Toyota. So Toyota made the extraordinary investment in building all new state-of-the-art dealerships and service shops just for the Lexus. It built these facilities with the customer's desires in mind. But the facilities would only be perceived as good as the service personnel and service experience itself. So

Toyota provided training for all employees from receptionist to salesman, from service manager to mechanic. The common denominator in this extensive training was the customer experience. The focus—make it pleasant and, if possible, eliminate all frictional points of encounter.

Lexus keeps all their showrooms and the repair facilities clean enough to eat off the floor. They offer pick-up and delivery for even routine maintenance as another common practice. There are new (or like new) loaner cars for those who desire a car while theirs is in repair. Lexus goes one step further with follow-up phone calls, sporadic calls to see "how you like the car," and an 800 number for 24 hour road service just in case it is ever needed.

For years, customers had learned to accept less from car dealers. Research showed that Lexus not only ought to be able to achieve a 100% satisfaction level, they could exceed it without going overboard. Their definition of a perfect car experience was actually higher than the consumers'. So, Lexus aimed to deliver 110% while the consumer expected 85%. The result—extraordinary customer satisfaction. Of course, it helps when your product is a state-of-the-art, very low maintenance, extraordinary quality automobile. And this high quality allowed extraordinary promises be made through advertising, promotion and publicity when the car was first introduced.

Here's another example of Lexus' 110% effort. A dealer phoned a customer shortly after the purchase to ask if anything was wrong. The customer was greatly pleased, the only thing wrong was "the wind noise from the phone antenna," he responded. When the customer went to get his car after the next maintenance visit (which was brought to the curb next to the door), he said, "that's not my car!" The service manager looked puzzled. "It's the same color and model, but the phone antenna is different and my car was coated with mud." The service manager smiled and said, "We contacted our technicians about that wind noise you referred to and they designed a new windless antenna. It's on us and we really appreciated your calling it to our attention. Also, it is our standard procedure to clean and vacuum your car before returning it to you." There are many more such stories from many other very satisfied customers.

Did this passion for customer service excellence pay off? You bet. Lexus was rated #1 for customer satisfaction the very first year it was measured, scoring the highest in the index of any car in history. Lexus sales soared in a down market, which was experiencing a particularly severe downtrend in the luxury car category. Lexus sales increased nearly 30 percent in its second year while its two primary established competitors experienced declines of as much as 34 percent and 27 percent. That's taking market share. Granted, some of the gain was due to value (quality at a fair and in this instance lesser price), but a lot of it was due and continues to be due to customer satisfaction.

Lexus knew the keys to winning new customers and is building a loyal base for repeat business with a highly fickle consumer group, and in a highly competitive industry. Lexus is succeeding with sales and marketing savvy closely integrated with a never before offered level of customer service. Except Lexus to remain rated the very best for a long time.

TURNER BROADCASTING/CNN

The first serious challenge to the major television news networks since their establishment—the Huntley-Brinkley days—has come from Cable News Network. Launched by Ted Turner in 1980, CNN provides up-to-date, sometimes up-to-the-minute, news coverage. TV news is expected to be timely, accurate, and in-depth. CNN is as accurate and in-depth as their competition, and they can be about as instantaneous as humanly possible. We all recall their extraordinary coverage of the Gulf War in early 1991.

CNN has been setting the pace as far back as 1981 when they scooped the major networks with the first reporting of an assassination attempt on President Reagan. Since then, CNN has won the battle for market share against extraordinary odds and competition by being there first with its around the clock and frequently live coverage as major events are taking place in the United States and around the world.

CNN has grown from a small cable news effort that reached just under two million households in its first year of operation, to a global audience which highly respects CNN and looks to them for the unfolding stories of the world. In fact, governments depend on its service and reporting for up-to-date information—which occasionally is better than that gathered by their intelligence services. Examples include the dramatic changes in the Soviet Union in 1991, the Gulf War, and developments in China in 1989.

CNN's services included not only Headline News, but also CNN World Report, CNN Newsource, CNN Newsroom, World Today, Sports, Science and Technology Week, Crossfire, Larry King Live, and Moneyline as of this writing. Each serves market segments with the best in its respective format areas. CNN is constantly improving their coverage, often with exclusive camera positions, interviews and firsts. It continues its growth in global expansions and market penetration. As the major networks are experiencing declines in viewership and scramble for answers and advertisers, CNN takes both market share and new ad revenue. In 1988, CNN further expanded to meet market needs with a Spanish version of Headline News.

CNN, because of its customer satisfaction through performance, has marketing momentum. Even the other media reinforce its performance, noting CNN's successes and attributable coverage. CNN has also done an excellent job of marketing itself. Ted Turner, the brains behind CNN was named Man of the Year by Time Magazine, largely because of the way CNN had changed the world of news.

There are numerous lessons we can learn from

CNN. First, CNN positioned their service offering to be distinct from other network news programs. They attracted competent, enthusiastic, and self-motivated employees. Further, CNN reinvested in itself to continually improve and remain ahead of competition. It introduced new programming and formats to retain viewers and allow for direct viewer feedback. CNN also understands the value of brand marketing as it trumpets the CNN brand in its commercials, through its leadership both in reporting as well as management, maintaining high visibility with the marketplace, and most of all, meeting the needs of its customers. CNN is unusual in that they have two disparate groups of customers: advertisers and viewers (including businesses like hotels) who pay for cable TV. CNN meets both the viewers' needs with the most objective and simply best news and its advertisers' needs by often going beyond expectations.

CNN cannot make the news, so they are dependent on outside events being interesting enough to create a quality broadcast everyday. Still, by hiring top-notch people, and investing more dollars than any other TV or radio company in the news, they are the best-prepared company to meet the needs of all their customers.

SUMMARY

What are the messages from these case examples? What constitutes being the best at quality service and winning customers in good times and bad?

One message that comes across is each firm has made quality a formal focus through either their leadership or a formal plan. AT&T and BP exemplify this concept.

Another common element is listening to the customers. Most look for reconditioning and the attitudes expressed in the marketplace and respond with specific new or improved service and/or marketing approaches. Think about CNN's programming and delivery, or Avis's express check-in program. Understanding the customers' needs certainly qualifies as a second important message.

Each winner reads the pulse of its marketplace through feedback from the customers and employees. Feedback mechanism, be they quality teams, customer surveys, employee suggestion processes, or a formal market research are in place in each case. Banc One's multiple feedback mechanisms and Stouffer Hotels' comprehensive guest relations program shine in this category.

Regardless of the size of the organization from the huge multi-nationals such as Toyota, AT&T and BP to the smaller L.L. Bean and Davis Frame Company—indeed, down to your local newspaper stand or coffee shop—employees at the point of encounter are the critical element. Each recognizes this and focuses upon these employees with support and motivational programs.

Striving to be the best also means communicating with both the consumer and within the organization. The winners read the signals sent by their customers (character types, market segments, etc.) and reply with timeliness, adjust their responses to the needs, and know what to say and what not to say.

This communication includes an interrelationship between customer service and sales and marketing. The focal point is managing a strong marketing message, but not promising more than operations can delivery. AT&T and American Express exemplify global competency in their delivery examples.

Each of the best understands the value of customer retention. Keeping existing customers through marketing programs, motivational service performance, and flexibility at the point of encounter through empowerment also stands out as a clear message from the best. Getting that Radisson "Yes I Can" attitude to become an ongoing behavior or the Avis "We Try Harder" to be felt by the customer brings them back for repeat encounters.

Recognition of the changing marketplace and competition and responding with service and sales strategies which bring in trial business taking customers from competitors is another common thread that binds the best. BP America didn't just survive their extraordinary image change, they thrived; Pearle's revolutionary guarantee of your glasses in less than 60 minutes made them the market winners.

Winners also share the common thrust of being on the forefront of innovation, be it through technological research and development, or through utilization of a good employee or customer-suggested process for improvement. Lexus, AT&T

and American Express understand that improvements and change are essential to ongoing competitiveness.

In the final analysis, quality service and sales excellence always comes down to the point of encounter. Every employee, every boss is a salesperson. Those who meet their customers' needs win not only that sale, but the sale after that, and the sale after that. Those who fail at the point of encounter lose not only their existing customer base, but have to work even harder to convince the next customer. Winners understand this simple principle and focus their resources to support their point-of-encounter employees. And they recognize that every sale, every customer, is the most important of all.

Let's recap the key points with respect to what constitutes the best at quality service and winning customers in good times and bad.

Winning Ingredients

- Leadership
- Formalized process or plan
- Focus on understanding customer needs
- Customer and employee feedback systems
- Responding with action on the feedback
- Sales and service synergy
- Customer-retention motivational and promotional programs
- Reading the marketplace and competition and responding appropriately
- Practicing innovation through research and development and suggestion implementation
- Prominent recognition of the importance of point-of-encounter employees and giving them full support

CONCLUSION

In the pre-service industry driven economy, the four "p's" (product, price, place, and promotion) were considered the keys to success in winning customers. While these key ingredients remain important, in this decade, the focus must essentially include:

1. recognizing customer needs
2. clearly communicating the relationship between the product/service offering and these needs
3. providing the incentive, motivation or rationale to convert the consumer to customer

4. personalizing the point-of-encounter interface.

A winning business understands the cost/benefit economics of customer retention. Better service increases prices directly or indirectly. At a certain point, the higher price diminishes demand. You have to find the optimum level of service that will meet the customers' needs at a price they are willing to pay. Also, the longer you retain an existing customer or the higher the repeat purchase factor in your mix of business, the greater the profit.

It is essential to understand where customers are coming from. What are their pre-purchase attitudes? Identifying their attitudes and their characteristics allows for proper response and sales strategy. Further, recognizing customer characteristics (customer types) and reading the signals each sends, is prerequisite to appropriate point-of-encounter responses. In order to know and keep customers, we must know when to reply, how to respond, how to read signals, and what to say or not say to each customer type.

Winning new customers and taking customers from your competition requires marketing strategy. This strategy is dynamic, based on demand in relationship to supply and factoring trend directions. To achieve market share gains and sales increases requires selecting the right strategy based on your product/service positioning in relationship to both market movement and competition. Often, different techniques are required in different market conditions.

The art of winning involves a service and sales synergy. Recognition of the point of encounter and employee behavior at this juncture is critical to sales success. Training programs, motivational programs, targeted internal and external communications, customer and employee feedback mechanisms, methods of strategy adjustment, and follow-up procedures all can help keep employees at their best.

The best at the art of winning understand the needs of their customers and strive to meet or exceed this norm. The best infuse all levels of workers with its commitment to customer satisfaction. The best invest in all areas critical to the point of encounter to make their product or service delivery preferred by the customer. The best understand their greatest asset in achieving success is the point-of-encounter employee. The best have a comfortable service attitude and make sure that no matter how "high-tech" the process, it remains a "high-touch" experience for the consumer. An experience where their slogans, be it "We Try Harder," "Whatever It Takes," or "Yes I Can," are practiced as standard modus operandi and understood by all employees. The best recognize customer satisfaction is a factor in job evaluation and so reward thoughts perform well. And finally, the best make the quality process and the marketing execution ongoing, changing with the needs of the customer and demand in the marketplace.

POST SCRIPT

• In the beginning . . .
Marketing creates the perceptions which are shaped into consumer expectations and the product/service promise is conceived.

• In between . . .
People seek to fulfill this promise at all the points of encounter with the consumer, who is nourished along the delivery system to the purchasing decision.

• In the end . . .
Quality is the consumers' assessment and opinion on expectations being met or exceeded. If the

verdict is positive, the consumer becomes a customer.

• Above the line . . .
No matter what *we* think, quality is what the *customer* perceives.

• Bottom line . . .
Exceeding expectations keeps customers in good times and bad.